W. H. (William Hartley) Carnegie

Through conversion to the creed

Being a brief account of the reasonable character of religious conviction

W. H. (William Hartley) Carnegie

Through conversion to the creed
Being a brief account of the reasonable character of religious conviction

ISBN/EAN: 9783741174490

Manufactured in Europe, USA, Canada, Australia, Japa

Cover: Foto ©Andreas Hilbeck / pixelio.de

Manufactured and distributed by brebook publishing software
(www.brebook.com)

W. H. (William Hartley) Carnegie

Through conversion to the creed

THROUGH CONVERSION
TO THE CREED

THROUGH CONVERSION TO THE CREED

Being a Brief Account of the Reasonable
Character of Religious Conviction.

BY

W. H. CARNEGIE, B.A.

RECTOR OF GREAT WITLEY, WORCESTERSHIRE

LONDON

LONGMANS, GREEN, & CO.

AND NEW YORK: 15 EAST 16th STREET

1893

PREFACE

THE following pages are intended to indicate a line of thought which the author has found satisfactory to himself, and which he hopes may prove useful to some others. They are an attempt to describe very briefly the origin and development of religious faith in the soul, and to show that there is nothing in them which reason cannot accept. Only the broadest outlines are touched upon ; but if the account given of them is accurate so far as it goes, it may possibly supply a framework into which others, who have not time or opportunity for mental self-analysis, can fit their own religious experiences and their own conceptions of truth, and thus aid them in arriving at a more connected and proportionate view of the different elements of their moral and spiritual life.

Such a result would have more than an intellectual importance : for a man's belief, if it is a real belief, is a summary of the principles and motives of his conduct; and it is of no small practical advantage for him to have a clear conception of the proportion which its different constituents bear to each other, and of the relations in which they stand to the intellectual life as a whole.

Without some such conception he is at the mercy of chance circumstances and sudden impulses : has no intellectual safeguard against extreme views or destructive criticisms : and is exposed to the danger on the one hand of losing his faith altogether, under the in-

fluence of tendencies apparently antagonistic
to it ; on the other of developing it in a
one-sided and mutilated manner, and thus
arriving at a chance combination of senti-
ments and prejudices, which is often little
less than a caricature of the Catholic Creed.

This danger is by no means an imaginary
one.   Our own country, with its hundreds of
hostile sects, each claiming to be the de-
pository of the complete truth: with its wide-
spread agnosticism and indifferentism : and
with its resulting train of wasted lives and
mutually destructive efforts, is a convincing
commentary on its reality.

Such a state of things can hardly be
looked upon as even an imperfect realization
of the apostolic ideal of the Catholic Church:
all-embracing, all-satisfying, all-complete; the
source and home of harmonious belief and

well-balanced action : the great Body "fitly
joined together and compacted by that which
every joint supplieth, according to the
effectual working in the measure of every
part."

How far the considerations brought forward by the author will commend themselves
to other minds differently constituted, it is
impossible for him to judge.   But even if
their rejection stimulates those minds to a
different method of attaining the object at
which they aim, the time and thought spent
on them will not have been wasted.

CONTENTS

I.

INTRODUCTORY.

TREATISES on Christian evidences for the most part begin with the assumption of doubt; with the assumption that those to whom they are addressed are conscious of definite and serious difficulties in the way of belief—difficulties which it is the endeavour of such treatises to remove; and if the endeavour is successful, as no doubt it often is, no further justification for Christian apology of this kind is needed.

But the assumption itself is by no means capable of universal application. There are some for whom doubt is a state of mind of

B

which they have had no conscious experience; for whom religion is not a thing that needs proof at all: being something rather which has grown with their growth, which has intertwined itself with the very essence of their being. A development, indeed, they may be able to trace in their religious conceptions; but it is a development which has run parallel with their other conceptions, intellectual and moral. The two, as they look back on their mental history, seem to have reacted on each other; to have advanced together in one organic growth, in which it is impossible to distinguish with anything like accuracy the different parts, or to analyze the relations that hold good between them.

Their case is, perhaps, in this age of controversy and criticism, rather exceptional; but there are many others, possibly the

majority of professing and conforming Christians, who, though they are not free from
what we may call implicit doubt, have never
had to enter into a life-and-death struggle
with it for the maintenance of their faith.
They may have always conformed to the
traditional system in which they have been
brought up, and found what they needed
of religious satisfaction in it ; or they may
have gradually adapted themselves to the
teaching and practice of the Church under
the influence of Christian literature or companionship ; or they may have identified
themselves with it as a whole, through the
vivid realization of the satisfaction which it
affords to some keenly felt want. But so
far as their intellects are concerned, their
religious development has been to a large
extent an untroubled one, with no striking

episodes, no strongly marked incidents. The creed, so far as they have realized its significance, has been accepted by them as the expression of their ideals and aspirations; so far as they have not so realized it, they are content to acknowledge its validity on the testimony of others, whose religious experience has been more extended than their own. Doubts they may have experienced about this doctrine or that, but only in a transient form, passing away like summer clouds, and leaving the main stream of their belief untouched; deep questionings may have suggested themselves from time to time, but they too have passed by without being answered, and without leaving any apparent results.

By such people evidences for Christianity, in the ordinary sense of the word, would perhaps be considered unnecessary. Their belief, they will say, is its own evidence. To ask them *why* they believed would be all one with asking why they thought, or felt, or desired ; why their nature is of such a kind and not of another. " I believe because I *do* believe," would be their immediate answer ; " because it is my nature to believe ; because I cannot help believing ; because thought, or action, or rational consciousness itself, without belief, would be to me a contradiction in terms. My belief is an integral part of my very nature, inseparable from it, intertwined with it. Why this should be so, He alone can tell from whose hands that nature came ; for my part, I am only concerned with using it in the best way possible, and developing it according to its own proper laws."

But however strong his conscious assurance may be, even the most convinced
Christian cannot afford to wholly neglect
the intellectual bearings of his belief, its
rational grounds and justification. Those
passing doubts and difficulties of which all
but a favoured few are conscious from time
to time, in a greater or less degree, though
they may dissolve away of their own accord
and leave the faith undisturbed, cannot be
completely disregarded. They are indications, so far as they go, that that faith has
not been brought into complete harmony
with the other experiences and convictions
of the mental and moral consciousness; that
the relation between it and them has not
been fully explored, but that it stands to a
certain extent in isolation. This isolation,
the believer may feel to be only apparent,

not real ; but a demand, emanating from the very depths of his consciousness, leads him to desire something more than a feeling in this respect—leads him to desire a conscious knowledge of the related coherence of his intellectual, moral, and spiritual conceptions. Such a demand will assert itself with greater or less strength when facts or theories are brought before his notice which profess to have a bearing on religious belief—a bearing either of antagonism or support ; and instinctively there will arise a craving for unity, a desire that these facts should be brought into harmony with those other deeper facts in which the foundations of his life lie hid ; that their interrelation and intercommunication should be made manifest. That such a harmony exists, and *can* be brought to light, he does not for an instant doubt; his only doubt is as to whether he individually has the opportunities of time and ability necessary for its accomplishment. But so long as any facts lie outside the range of that system of unified conscious thought which makes up what we call knowledge, so long there is a want felt; a want, it may be, which it will take eternity to satisfy, which the lack of opportunity or the exigencies of higher calls may deny even a partial satisfaction to in this world; but which nevertheless asserts its claim, and tends at any rate to the production of such action as will fulfil that claim.

Another reason why believing Christians cannot leave these arguments and theories out of account, is because of their manifest effect on others. One essential mark of religious growth is growth in sympathy. The more the religious faculty in a man develops itself, the more will he learn that his life is not self-centred, but that it is connected by innumerable ties with the lives of others ; that what affects them, must have an interest for him ; must be taken into account, if not for his own sake, yet for theirs. However little, then, these outer voices may affect him, he cannot disregard them, when he sees how different is their significance to others ; that to others they bring, it may be, messages of doubt or difficulty, or even despair. He is bound to listen to them, in order to see how far they can be brought into harmony with that master-strain which he would have all learn ; how far they have to be rejected as inconsistent with it. His very religion forces him to take cognizance of them, and to find for them their due place.

Now, to a state of mind such as has been indicated, the following pages are addressed. They do not seek to justify the facts of religion, still less to prove them. But, assuming the existence of those facts and the recognition of their vital reality, an attempt will be made to give a unified expression to them; to show their relations to each other, and to indicate the lines on which they may be embodied in a systematized whole. And the method of the attempt will be as follows. First, the act of faith itself will be considered, and an endeavour will be made to show that it is not an irrational act; but that in itself, in its process and in the conditions which it implies, it is in the highest degree rational, if by rationality we mean that power by which we discover new truths, advance in know-

ledge, and guide our conduct in the practical concerns of everyday life. And then,
secondly, the act itself having thus been
given its place among recognized mental
operations, a further endeavour will be made
to show how it necessarily develops itself
into an outward expression of a particular
kind : how, in other words, the expression
given to it in the creeds and system of the
Catholic Church is not a mere extraneous
clothing, but something which in its own
very nature it implies ; something, indeed,
added from without, but, when once added,
responded to with such an intensity of
recognition that it becomes no longer an
addition, but an integral part of faith's own
organic growth.

Such an attempt, thus stated, may appear
a very ambitious one, and one which would

need no slight aid both from metaphysics and from the philosophy of history for its complete success. But these deep waters we need not venture into. Our appeal is made to the ordinary well-educated believer: to the man who, though he may not have been trained to the discussion of the ultimate problems of thought and existence, still has a well-balanced mind; is able to appreciate the intellectual bearings of most questions; is able to pass judgment on most subjects of practical importance; is able with fair accuracy and confidence to discriminate the true from the false in what concerns his life's interests and wants. For such a man metaphysical discussions have no practical significance; his ordinary beliefs and certitudes and convictions are gained or lost altogether independently of metaphysics; and if his religious belief can be shown to be on a level with these, it is all that his intellectual conscience can require. For such a man, it will be sufficient to begin where metaphysics leaves off. All that he can legitimately want, is that his religious belief should be brought into unity with the rest of his mental experiences; that considerations of a like kind and of a similar level should be seen to hold good for both. Anything beyond that, anything needing deeper or more subtle trains of thought, he may well dispense with; may well leave to the learned few, for whom alone they can have anything more than a mere theoretical interest.

II.

THE NATURE OF FAITH.

OUR first object, then, must be to understand, so far as we can, the nature of faith ; of that activity of the soul which underlies all religious belief, and alone makes it possible. And, in order to do so, we must begin by putting to one side all so-called dogmatic definitions. These, however useful in themselves, are not applicable here ; since our appeal is made, not to professed theologians, but to ordinary believers, who, though keenly alive to the *facts* of their religious consciousness, have never analyzed those facts nor arranged them in a coherent plan.

Rather, then, let us turn to that religious consciousness itself, and try to describe what it is that takes place there at the time when the act of faith is perhaps most clearly recognized, at the time of what people call *conversion*.

Conversion, in the sense of a definite and intensely realized change in the religious attitude of the mind at some particular time, though not a universal experience, is far from an exceptional one, still further from being an abnormal one. Indeed, it is perhaps not too much to say, that conversion in some sense of the word *is* a universal experience among those to whom religion is a reality. It may not come, probably in the majority of cases does not come, as a sudden event, but rather by way of a consecutive process, the successive stages of which are so gradually achieved that it is almost impossible to distinguish them from each other. Still the result is the same : the man who can say "I believe," and give these words their full religious significance, is conscious of a changed attitude of mind, of an achievement of vital moment in the domain of religious thought and action. Our appeal here is to religious people, and those only; to people to whom religion, in the deeper sense of the word, is a reality. The facts of their experience are our premises; and I think we are justified in assuming that, among those facts, the fact of conversion holds a prominent place; that none of them would deny it to be true of themselves in some sense of the word ; that they would all agree that a change has taken place in their attitude towards spiritual things—a change gradual or sudden, but one which has affected vitally the deepest issues of life for them : has given to wants a promise of complete satisfaction ; to aspirations, an all-embracing ideal ; to tendencies and impulses and affections, which seemed before to lead anywhere or nowhere, a unity of meaning and purpose capable of holding them together in one system, harmonious and complete.

Assuming this, then—and though the assumption is a weighty one, I think we are justified in making it—our analysis of the act of faith would resolve itself into an analysis of the fact of conversion. For there, perhaps, faith shows itself in its most potent activity ; and, for the sake of greater distinctness, we will take that particular form of conversion in which this activity is most intensely realized ; in which the change which takes place is an immediate one ;

C

the steps of the process being, as it were, combined, and brought under the vivid light of a concentrated mental experience.

One prominent example of such a conversion is given to us in the New Testament ; and though some of the characteristics of that conversion are unique, it will, I think, in its main outlines, serve as a type of all, and will readily be admitted as such by those who have passed through a similar change.

Let us, then, try to understand something of that process which changed Saul, the persecuting Pharisee, into Paul, the zealous Christian believer.

Saul, by nature and education, was evidently what we should call of an intensely religious temperament. He sprang from a religious stock—a Pharisee of the Pharisees—

and all his natural tendencies were fostered
and developed by the education he received.
Brought up at the feet of Gamaliel, he
imbibed there all that was best and clearest
and most systematized in the religious
thought of his time. Nor did this education
make him a mere theologian, a mere specu-
lator on spiritual facts, a mere co-ordinator
of spiritual theories. With him, life was an
intensely practical thing; thought was only
valuable so far as it could be translated into
action. So, taking as his working theory of
life that system of things in which Provi-
dence had placed him, he began to apply it
with all the energy of his nature to the
practical problems with which he found
himself confronted. How far or how long
that application proved satisfactory to him,
we can only conjecture. At what stage of

the process he began to have misgivings as
to its validity, lurking doubts stifled for the
time by redoubled zeal, but bound to re-
assert themselves again when opportunity
offered itself. It may have been that as he
watched the martyred Stephen, his face
illumined with the glory of another world,
a ray from that glory penetrated to him,
and brought with it a glimpse of something
higher and nobler and more soul-satisfying
than the traditional system to which he had
pledged himself; it may have been that
as he harried the simple Nazarene peasants
and haled them to prison, the sight of their
simple confident faith awakened the question whether, after all, they had not reached
a deeper stratum of truth than that which
needed to be guarded by the logic of the
schools and the power of penal enactments.

But however the awakening came, come it did. "It is hard for thee," said the Divine Voice, "to kick against the pricks." Dissatisfaction is implied there—dissatisfaction deep-rooted and potent; obtruding itself at unexpected moments; impeding the course of single-minded action; turned away from, beaten down with determined zeal, but emerging again when the storm had passed; checking the current of mistaken life, forcing it to seek some truer channel for its activity. Thus we may conjecture was it with the apostle, as he started on that memorable ride to Damascus; thus has it been with thousands of souls since, on the eve of their conversion. He felt, though he fain would not acknowledge it, that the old footholds of his life were beginning to slip away from beneath him; he was prepared, though he hardly perhaps knew it himself, to take his stand on other firmer ground, and thence to view the world anew.

The time had come; the way of the Lord had been prepared; the Lord Himself advances to meet the earnest though misguided soul. "Saul, Saul, why persecutest thou Me?" "Who art Thou, Lord?" "I am Jesus of Nazareth whom thou persecutest." "Jesus of Nazareth"—it was no new name to his ears. A name, indeed, of infamy and contempt among those whose agent he was, but a name which could not but awaken many a lingering echo of a far different kind—echoes of which the very air of Palestine was full; tales of wonderful works of power performed, of boundless sympathy and compassion shown; reports of soul-stirring sayings going to the very heart of things—of terrible privations unwaveringly undergone ; of unflinching steadfastness in persecution and betrayal ; of calm complacency at the hour of trial ; of unswerving dignity and courage in that of death ; of nature's response to that climax of the life ; of the heavens darkened ; of the graves opening and giving up their dead ; of the veil of the temple rent in twain.

All this, and much more than this, must the name have connoted for him, as he lay there prostrate on the ground ; and now for the first time its true significance burst upon him. Tendencies long suppressed asserted themselves ; wants long felt clamoured for satisfaction, and no longer found it denied ; ideals treated before as fantastic dreams, emerged into active reality ; sympathies and affections restrained hitherto within the bounds of a narrow ecclesiasticism, rushed forth in unimpeded freedom ; the whole energy of the soul had found an adequate field for its development ; all the innumerable potentialities of heart and spirit and intellect had found channels for their activity ; the whole nature, with its infinity of interwoven capacities and requirements, concentrated itself in one grand act of recognition and response ; it had found that without which it could never be complete ; had touched that to which it could instinctively attach itself ; no mere ideal, no abstract theory of life ; but a living personality with which all the fibres and nerves and sinews of the man's own personality could unite themselves in one organic growth. In identifying himself with that Personality, in becoming one with It, that which he had sought, perhaps unconsciously, these many years, had been found ; the true solution of life's problem had been attained ; the man was converted.

In thus describing St. Paul's conversion, we have tried to do so in the most general terms, omitting so far as possible what was peculiar to his case, and dwelling rather on its common characteristics. Thus to St. Paul undoubtedly the revelation of Christ came primarily as the revelation of the Messiah ; and his acceptance of Him would present itself in the first instance as the acceptance of One who had fulfilled the prophecies of the Old Testament, and who would in His own good way, though that an unexpected way, establish the Kingdom of God on earth. But the Messiahship and the Kingdom were but signs and tokens ; the range of ideas which they contained was as much wider than that

of Old Testament aspiration as the Christian
ideal is wider than the Jewish; and the
appeal to which the apostle responded, just
because it transcended and seemed to contradict the anticipations engendered by his
Pharisaic antecedents, must have been
relative to universal human wants and
aspirations which Pharisaism left unsatisfied.
The spiritual basis of the man who wrote
the Epistle to the Corinthians must have
been as broad as the religious consciousness
itself; and it is not an illegitimate procedure
to eliminate from the account of his conversion
its accidental and transient features, and to
treat it as a type of all. At the bar of
that consciousness, then, we present this
account of the climax fact in its history; a
fact, indeed, of infinite complexity and
mystery; a process of which the successive

stages are often barely, if at all, recognized at the time ; a result attained by way of instinctive, spontaneous recognition rather than by that of self-conscious thought, but nevertheless capable to a certain extent of being analyzed and described. If this analysis and description represent, however inadequately, an experience which believers will recognize as true in its main outlines of themselves, their object has been attained.

The act of faith, though, does not end at conversion. There a master-principle of life is brought to light, a solution of its mysterious difficulty offered ; but that principle has to be tested, that solution has still to be shown to be adequate to the facts of the case. Failing such test, it remains only an exceptional phenomenon, an emotional episode nowise related to the reality of things.

Conversion may, according to the point of view from which we regard it, be described as the acceptance of an all-embracing ideal, as the solution of a life-problem, or as the satisfaction of a complex system of wants and aspirations. Its adequacy in these respects is guaranteed at the time by an act of spontaneous recognition; an act accompanied by a feeling of security and repose, which seems to attest its validity. But the contents of the recognition have to be examined before this validity is assured. The ideal must be seen to be adequate, not merely to those conditions which the circumstances of the special occasion made prominent, but to all the conditions of the case; the solution must not merely meet some special difficulties in the problem, but all difficulties; the satisfaction must be relative, not merely to the wants and aspirations of the particular time, but to all such as from time to time had asserted themselves. Moreover, the future has to be considered as well as the present and the past. Other conditions may arise, other difficulties may present themselves; other wants and aspirations may assert themselves, and demand their satisfaction; and these in turn will have to be provided for. The contents of the recognition will have to be unfolded in relation to them, and a place found for their legitimate demands in its ordered unity.

Thus a twofold test has to be applied: an intellectual test, proceeding by way of reflective self-analysis; and a practical test, consisting in the application of the new-found principle to the exigencies and difficulties of ordinary life.

Of course, neither of these tests could be applied exhaustively. The most intense reflection could never exhaust the hidden depths of want and aspiration which each man finds in his soul; the clearest intellect could hardly hope to analyze all the necessary conditions of their satisfaction; while the test of practical efficiency, the *solvitur ambulando* test, would, from the nature of the case, not be complete till life itself, with all its varied circumstances and contingencies, had passed into eternity.

But in proportion to time, to opportunity, and to ability, the first test must be applied, if a haunting sense of insecurity is to be avoided. Pressing difficulties, at any rate, must be accounted for and solved; the most powerful wants, at any rate, must be met with adequate satisfaction; the deepest

currents of life, at any rate, must be given
an outlet through which they can more easily
and freely flow into ever-widening channels.
And in the same way, as life unfolds itself,
the principle must unfold itself too ; must
show by its growth and adaptability that it
is a living principle ; must give increasing
promise of capacity and power ; must supply
that which is needed from day to day of
direction and guidance and strength.

Now, both these tests St. Paul applied, as
perhaps no converted man has ever applied
them since. For three years, we are told,
he went into solitary retirement into the
desert of Arabia ; and those three years,
we can hardly be wrong in assuming, were
spent in intense reflection and meditation ;
in bringing all the different elements of his
moral and intellectual nature into relation

with the new life which had opened out on him; in systematizing them, and finding for each of them its due place. From that retirement he emerged with triumphant confidence. The Vision of Beauty was no mere dream; it had proved its reality and its worth; it was no longer an unrelated phenomenon, but had expanded on all sides until it had included the whole nature in a conscious unity of expression. The fact of conversion had stood the first test of reflection and analysis, and, in doing so, had developed itself into an exhaustive system of theology. To this system he now proceeded to apply the further test of practical efficiency. Would it hold its own when brought face to face with the practical exigencies of active life? Would it still supply the satisfaction of which it gave

promise under the trying ordeal of daily
effort ? The answer to these questions is
written in letters of fire, in the story of his
apostolic life: " In journeyings often, in perils
of waters, in perils of robbers, in perils by
mine own countrymen, in perils by the
heathen, in perils in the city, in perils in the
wilderness, in perils in the sea, in perils
among false brethren ; in weariness and
painfulness, in watchings often, in hunger
and thirst, in fastings often, in cold and
nakedness. Beside those things which are
without, that which cometh upon me daily,
the care of all the churches."

Such is the summary of a life, unique
perhaps in its hardness and varied difficulty
of experience ; such was the ordeal by which
the divine principle was tested. And the
result ? " I am persuaded that neither death,

D

nor life, nor angels, nor principalities, nor powers, nor things present, nor things to come, nor height, nor depth, nor any other creature, shall be able to separate us from the love of God, which is in Jesus our Lord."

The last remnant of doubt had vanished ; the last possibility of hesitation had been swept away ; the deepest depths had been sounded ; the most trying circumstances, the fiercest opposition, the bitterest persecution, had hurled their forces against his stronghold in vain. The life-principle had but strengthened itself through them all, and now swept him on in readiness for the eternity from which it sprang. "I know Whom I have believed, and am persuaded that He is able to keep that which I have committed unto Him against that day." It is the triumph-song of victorious faith.

The vicissitudes of the world could no longer affect his inner calm any more than the storm on the surface of the ocean can affect the depths beneath. Before him stretched out an illimitable prospect, in which death was but an episode; but a dissolving of those conditions which limited his complete development; but a rending of a veil interposed between his aspirations and their full fruition in the eternal order of reality.

Now let us sum up these results. The process of faith, as thus exemplified in a typical instance, consists in—

(1) A preliminary training or discipline, presupposing certain faculties and capacities to be trained, and resulting in a certain mental attitude of receptiveness, a recognition of certain wants and a wish to satisfy them.

(2) The attempt to satisfy these wants, to meet these aspirations. This attempt is made in the first instance spontaneously and instinctively; the mind, as it were, feels around it for the satisfaction it requires, and comes back bringing with it some new acquisition which promises such satisfaction.

The method of the attempt when reflected on afterwards is thus seen to be the method of hypothesis; of taking some proffered solution, and seeing whether it will meet the conditions of the case. Several such hypotheses may be tried before the true one is attained; but the successive failure of those which are found to be inadequate defines the object of the search, for it brings the necessary conditions of the problem into clearer relief, and by a process of exclusion concentrates the attention on them.

(3) The true hypothesis at length is attained, and the mind at once responds to it by an instinctive act of recognition, accompanied by a feeling of satisfaction and completion.

(4) This act is found, on examination, to be one of self-recognition ; that is to say, the mind recognizes its new acquisition as a thing co-natural with itself : a development of its own capabilities and powers, or such of them as asserted themselves most strongly at the time the act was made.

(5) This self-recognition is carried further still by reflection and self-analysis ; until all those capabilities which had as yet emerged into consciousness are met by possible lines of development.

(6) Further still, it unfolds itself in relation to those which the varying experiences of life elicit : the hypothesis is seen to hold

good for them as well—to direct their aims, to meet their aspirations, to harmonize their conflicting claims.

(7) Thus faith gradually approximates to certainty ; the hypothetical element in it gradually diminishes ; the *whole* self becomes gradually related to another Self, and as its gaze concentrates there, every energy of its nature unites in hastening forward the advance towards complete union with that Other in which alone they will find their full field of development.

III.

THE ANALOGY OF FAITH.

IF the account we have given of the process of faith is in its main outlines a true account, however inadequate it may be, the next question which calls for our consideration is this: Is the process as thus described *sui generis?* Is it a unique phenomenon in the history of a man's mental and moral experiences, standing by itself, unrelated to anything else? Or is it, on the contrary, comparable to other processes by which knowledge is attained, and action is governed; differing from them, indeed, in the vast subject-matter with which it is concerned, in the eternal issues which it involves, and in the source from which the energy of its action flows, but in its method and form analogous to them, starting from a similar basis, proceeding by similar steps, applying similar tests, arriving at similar mental results ?

If the latter be the true answer, it will be impossible to deny that faith—so far, at any rate, as its method and form are concerned, is a rational process ; and by bringing its operation to this extent, within the province of recognized mental acts, the first step will be taken towards that conscious perception of unity which our nature craves, and which it is our present object to attain.

With this object in view, then, let us take one or two typical instances of processes which all would recognize as rational, and try in the briefest outline to trace their successive steps.

(1) Take the most simple, as being the most abstract instance of all—the process by which we solve a problem in geometry.

First, then, certain preliminary conditions are necessary before we approach the consideration of such a problem at all. We must have been trained to a certain extent in geometrical habits of thought ; must know what a problem of this kind means ; and must, indeed, have certain facts of a similar nature which we already acknowledge as true : facts not isolated from each other, but forming part of a related whole, which is capable of extending itself to all facts of that particular kind. Moreover, this capability must be recognized, and the instinctive wish to satisfy it, to make the whole complete, is the motive power which sets the mind in action in any direction which would seem to lead towards the attainment of its object.

Next, the particular problem is presented to the mind thus prepared, and it proceeds to solve it. Its method in this process, whether consciously recognized as such or not, is purely one of hypothesis; it proposes a certain solution to itself—Suppose such and such is the true solution : will it satisfy the conditions of the case? The particular hypothesis, indeed, is not a random guess ; it is built up of materials supplied from previous experience and previous efforts of the same kind ; and its suitability will depend to a large extent upon the width of that experience and the intensity of those efforts. The practised geometrician will hit upon the true hypothesis at once ; the novice will perhaps try several before he does so.

When the true hypothesis has been attained, its correctness is at once recognized by a feeling of rest and satisfaction, which, though not an absolute guarantee of that correctness, is still a strong presumption in its favour.

This guarantee is supplied by reflection, by seeing that the given solution meets all the conditions of the case, and thus relates itself to that body of acknowledged truth which has already been attained. Such a test is very easily applied in this instance on account of the extremely abstract character of the subject-matter involved; the clearly marked and comparatively few lines of connection which bind it together; and the new fact is thus raised to the same level of certainty as that system of facts to which it is thus related ; certainty generally supposed to be of the highest kind, since such system depends upon intuitive truths—truths the opposite of which is unthinkable, and is related to them by laws of a similar kind. Hence we are assured of the validity of the new discovery, not merely with regard to all past discoveries, but with regard to all in the future as well, for any fact incompatible with it, would be incompatible with the foundation facts on which the whole system is based ; but since such incompatibility is unthinkable, the supposed fact is unthinkable, and therefore, so far, at any rate, as we are concerned, not a fact at all.

(2) The next instance which we would take is that of the discovery of a new law in physical science. Here again the steps

are identical with those already indicated;
the preliminary training resulting in a certain
aptitude of mind for such efforts, in certain
wants which need satisfaction, and in the
acquisition of a certain system of acknowledged facts homogeneous to the subject-
matter under consideration; then the hypothetical law, relating the new facts to the
old, its truth indicated by a feeling of satisfaction, but not guaranteed till the new
law is seen by reflection to hold good for
all the relations in which the given facts
are known to stand, *i.e.* till it is seen to
fit into that system of established laws which
constitute our recognized body of truth with
respect to facts of a similar kind. Moreover,
the guarantee can never be absolute, till
all such facts have been brought under
observation, an impossible condition to fulfil

in most cases. For in the physical world intuitive laws have no place, and even the foundation-laws on which the fabric of our physical knowledge rests are of a hypothetical character—are accepted as universally true because they are seen to hold good so far as observation has gone, and, moreover, hold good in like cases as they come under observation, enabling us to make predictions with regard to them which are afterwards verified. It is always possible, therefore, for a physical law to be contradicted by experience, and though that possibility recedes as the field of observation extends, it still always has to be taken into account. No physical law can ever be said to rise above the level of a high probability, and instances are not wanting of laws which were accepted for generations as true, but which had to be thrown aside as inadequate because of the discovery of facts incompatible with them. The emission theory of light is an instance in point.

(3) One more instance will be sufficient for our purpose—an instance taken from ordinary life — the method by which an ordinary man directs his practical conduct in the world, by which he guides his action under such and such circumstances.

Once more we can see the same process at work. He has been more or less trained in worldly affairs; has thus attained a standard of judgment with regard to them, a greater or less experience in dealing with them, certain principles which he wishes to observe with regard to them, and the recognition of certain wants which he wishes to satisfy through them. A certain set of circumstances is presented to him, and he has to make up his mind how he is to act with regard to them ; what the course of action is to be which will attain his ends, satisfy his wants, and carry out his principles. Again he makes a hypothesis ; a hypothesis more or less good in proportion to his ability, experience, and practical power ; but a hypothesis still. He puts before him a certain course of action, and considers, so far as he is able, whether it is likely to be the right course ; whether it will meet the conditions of the case so far as he understands them. This consideration affords the first test of the hypothesis ; and if this holds good, he proceeds to apply the second—the test of practical application. Only when it has passed this second test, and the particular course of action is justified by its success, can it be said to have passed out of the probable stage. So long as it is in active operation as a principle of conduct, it cannot be more than a probability, though the probability is one which approaches more and more to certainty as its applicability gradually unfolds itself, and our trust in it may be indefinitely strengthened by the circumstances under which the conception of it was originally evolved; especially if those circumstances include the fact that it had received the imprimatur of some one of acknowledged authority and experience.

Here, then, are three typical instances of mental and practical activity to which no one would deny the title of rational; and though the account of the successive steps by which the mind proceeds in the attainment of its object is of the most meagre character, it

E

will answer our purpose if it is true so far
as it goes, since it shows that the process
is the same in all, and is, moreover, identical
with that by which the activity that we call
faith proceeds in the attainment of *its* object.
We are justified, then, in concluding that the
process of faith, so far as its *method* is concerned, is a purely rational process; and
thus far, at any rate, is not an isolated
phenomenon in mental experience, but can
be brought into relationship to and co-ordina-
tion with other examples of rational action;
and therefore presents no obstacle to the
satisfaction of that demand for unity in our
mental experiences which seems to be one
of the ultimate demands of our nature.

If, then, faith is irrational, it must be so
with regard to its subject-matter; with
regard to those experiences and that training

which form its conditions, which go to produce that attitude of mind and spirit in which the demand for faith naturally arises; or it must be irrational in the form which that demand takes, in the nature of the hypotheses to which it gives rise; or it must be irrational in the estimation of the evidence by which those hypotheses are transformed into undoubted facts. In other words, it must be irrational in its conditions, in its content or in its development.

Whether this is so, will be considered in the following chapters.

IV.

THE CONDITIONS OF FAITH.

ARE the conditions of faith irrational?
That is to say, is that particular attitude
of mind to which belief is possible and easy,
an attitude which is unsuitable for rational
action of any other kind; one which would
tend to prevent a man who assumes it
from freely exercising his reason on subject-
matters other than those directly religious?

In the first place, then, it is obvious that
some conditions are necessary; that there is
a certain attitude of mind which predisposes
to religious belief, and without which that
belief is, humanly speaking, impossible. This

fact is emphasized again and again through the New Testament. " He that hath ears to hear, let him hear ; " " He that is spiritually minded judgeth all things ; " " My sheep hear My voice, and I know them, and they follow Me ; " " He that willeth to do the will shall know of the doctrine, that it is of God ; " are but some examples of numerous statements which all emphasize the same teaching—the teaching that a certain preparation is necessary before the act of faith can be consciously exercised ; a preparation resulting in a certain attitude of receptiveness towards spiritual things; a readiness of response to their claims.

So far, no charge of irrationality can be made. Every exercise. of reason requires certain conditions for its successful operation ; conditions which vary with the subject-matter to which that exercise is relative. The question turns on the nature of these conditions; whether they are such as are likely to produce a rational attitude of mind; one which would not at any rate be hostile to the rational consideration of questions other than religious.

Now, the conditions of faith seem to be summed up in one statement of our Lord's, which, if we read it in the light of others of a similar import, will give us some conception of their nature. That statement is, "Whosoever shall not receive the kingdom of God as a little child, shall in no wise enter therein." And the context of the words reveals the line of interpretation which must be applied to them—the interpretation that what is necessary before the act of faith can be made is an attitude of mind such as is most commonly found in children ; a state of heart and intellect which has not been deteriorated by contact with lower natures, or by the ardent pressure of the struggle for material well-being, but retains that simplicity of thought and intention which characterizes the earlier stages of mental and moral growth.

If we unfold the contents of this conception by the aid of other statements bearing on the same subject, we shall get a fairly adequate idea of those characteristics of heart and mind which constitute the conditions of the act of faith, and shall be able to judge in detail of their character.

The first characteristic which suggests itself, and which, indeed, is brought into special prominence in the passage to which I have alluded, is that of submissiveness—

humility : " Whosoever shall humble himself, the same is greatest in the kingdom of heaven." And this requisite of heavenly citizenship is under different forms referred to again and again through the New Testament : *i.e.* " Blessed are the poor in spirit ; " " Blessed are the meek ; " " Thou hast hid these things from the wise and prudent, and hast revealed them unto babes ; " while it is one of the few facts with reference to our Lord's childhood which is marked with special emphasis, " That He was subject to His parents."

Now, this grace of humility, though essentially a Christian grace, and unrecognized before Christ came into the world, has become so familiar to us since its first exemplification in the Incarnate Life, that it has become part of our ordinary ideal of conduct, and any criticism on it, as a moral qualification for the right exercise of faith, would apply equally to any other article of the recognized moral code. One application of it, however, will not meet with such a ready acquiescence, and that is when its claim is asserted in the operations of the intellect. Intellectual humility is not fashionable nowadays; at any rate, intellectual humility in the discussion of religious questions, and in the attainment of religious truth. The general impression in such matters seems to be that only such truths are to be accepted as we have personally tested and verified by the intellectual process suitable to their peculiar character; that to accept any other facts as true than those which have passed through such an ordeal, is not merely irrational, but is morally indefensible. That in his religious belief, at any rate, each man must find out the truth for himself, and act up to such lights as are given to him ; nor will he be held responsible if, having done so, he falls short of a more complete truth attainable by other greater lights.

Such statements are true or false, according to the interpretation which we give them. If they are taken to mean that a man's conscience is his ultimate standard of right and wrong, whether as regards his religious beliefs or his actions, of course no exception can be taken to them, provided always that he recognizes the responsibility under which he lies for informing and training his conscience itself by every means in his power. But if they mean that only such beliefs are to be accepted as true, and acted on as such, as have been subjected by the individual himself to the highest scientific and critical tests of which they are capable, then they are not merely untrue, but absurd. For (1) the great mass of beliefs, practical and theoretical, that constitute the intellectual equipment of any individual, and about whose truth he has no doubt whatever—which form, indeed, the standard of reference by which he judges of other statements when presented to him for his acceptance—have been subjected by him to no such tests, nor indeed, from the nature of the case, could they be. Few men, if any, would have the ability to verify for themselves all the truths which go to make up even one department of knowledge, much less *all* such departments ; fewer still would have the time necessary for such an investigation, or, if they had, would be willing to spend it on such an unnecessary task. The real way in which the greater part of his stock of knowledge is attained is on the *authority* of others whose experience has been larger than his, and whose judgment in their own particular subject-matter is held in general repute. Their decision he accepts unhesitatingly; and even when he examines the steps by which that decision has been arrived at, he does so more for the sake of learning their method of research and gaining an implement of thought which will be useful in future investigations of a similar kind than with any idea of criticizing it. It is sufficient for him that this knowledge is accepted as sound and reliable by those who are competent to judge, and that, when apprehended by him, it shows itself capable of indefinite expansion in answer to his own efforts. If either of these conditions is lacking; if the conclusions of some particular thinker are viewed with general disfavour and distrust; or if something in his own experience seems to be absolutely irreconcilable and inconsistent with them;—then it is time enough to investigate the grounds of those conclusions, and to see, if possible, the flaw in them.

(2) Such a demand for an *ab initio* investigation into the reliability of all the facts which we acknowledge as true would carry us into very deep waters indeed, for it would involve the consideration, not only of those facts themselves, but of the methods by which we give a knowledge of any truth. These methods, though of course their roots lie in the ultimate constitution of our nature, so far as their form is concerned, owe a great

deal to education and to the external influences under which they have been developed ; and a comprehensive survey of the
genesis of our knowledge would have to
include those influences and that education
within its range—no easy matter, since the
instruments of thought which we should
have to use for such a purpose would be to
a large extent the production of the subject-
matter upon which they were employed.

(3) Even in such truths as we have investigated and tested for ourselves, the element of authority is not wanting ; for except
the subject-matter is of such a kind that we
can examine all the instances to which the
truth applies—and this can be but seldom
the case—we assume that it holds good in
the unexamined cases on the authority of
those we have investigated.

Since, then, in no department of thought or action can we be independent of the influence of others, since both our assumptions, our materials, and our methods are to a large extent accepted by us on authority, there is nothing irrational in making the recognition of this consideration a preliminary to the right exercise of thought, whether in religious matters or elsewhere. Indeed, such a recognition is made, consciously or unconsciously, by all serious students and all practical men of action. A novice at starting may think that he can deduce all thought and all conduct from intuitive truths; but a little experience will teach him that if his intellectual and moral life is not to be wasted, he must be contented with a far lower ambition—must be contented, for the most part, with applying laws which he has received on the authority of others, without spending too much time or effort in tracing them back to their original sources ; and his time will be fully occupied if he can conscientiously do this in relation to the new experiences and circumstances which his own life bring to light. Nor will he have any reason to feel that his function in life is not fully discharged, when by doing so he has added to the stock of human knowledge in extending the application and adding to the certainty of those great hypotheses which successive generations of thought have evolved. Should he try to act otherwise, and, throwing aside these hypotheses, attempt to start afresh in isolated effort, his intellect will lead him to nothing better than a disappointing dreamland, his actions to contradiction and absurdity.

A second characteristic which the analogy of the child-nature suggests is that of moral integrity—purity of heart and intention. We naturally think of a child as one whose moral nature is untainted by contact with evil, still retaining its simple directness of perception and judgment; whose sense of right and wrong is still keen and unblunted. And such an application of the analogy is supported by other statements in different parts of the New Testament; *e.g.* " Blessed are the pure in heart, for they shall see God;" "He that willeth to do His will shall know of the doctrine, whether it be of God."

Here, then, a second condition of faith, a second requisite for its right exercise, seems to be indicated. It must be relative to and grow out from a good moral disposition. Such a disposition forms part of the foun-

F

dation of its essential character. Lacking it, its action must be distorted and untrue, while the strength and directness of that action will depend upon the extent to which this condition is cultivated and developed.

That there is nothing irrational in such a condition goes without saying. All whose opinion is worthy of respect will admit the importance of the due cultivation of the moral nature, and, indeed, its absolute necessity, as a preliminary to a right attitude with regard to most questions of social and personal importance.

But though this may be admitted in words, the practical inference which follows from it is often disregarded or overlooked — the inference that a man who has not cultivated his moral nature to the utmost of his abilities and opportunities ; who has not tried to live up to the standard of good and right which he finds recognized in the society in which he lives ;—is, in proportion to his neglect in these respects, disqualified for the consideration of religious questions ; in that proportion lacks the experiences and tests upon which a right judgment in such matters is based, and is not conscious of the moral wants and aspirations which lead him beyond morality itself to seek their satisfaction in something higher.

To many a man who bewails the impossibility of belief in his particular case, who even takes up an attitude of hostile criticism towards the belief of others, the reply of St. Francis will apply: "If you lived as I live, you would believe as I believe."

These remarks apply still more strongly.

to a third characteristic which seems to be implied in the "childlike" attitude of mind, the characteristic of spiritual sensitiveness. A child is naturally more sensitive to spiritual impressions than a grown-up person. The sense of mystery is strong in him; his faculties have not yet been narrowed by concentration on material aims and ambitions; and the conception of an existence transcending that of the sensible world in which he lives, and using that world but as a symbol or mode of expression, is not merely easy, but is quite natural to him.

Such a temperament, when shown in later life, is apt to be treated with some disdain by those who are pleased to pose as the hardheaded, commonsense, rational men of sound, well-balanced judgment; is apt to be dismissed by them with some half-contemptuous phrase; and it is thought that sufficient has been said about it when, by identifying it with mere imagination or fancy, it has been assigned to that low and unimportant position in the scale of human faculties which such words seem to imply.

But a little consideration will show the injustice of such a criticism. If by imagination we mean the faculty which enables us to rise above the experiences of sense, and to catch glimpses of the hidden meaning which they contain; to combine them into new self-formed experiences; to follow out the indications which they convey into regions which transcend all sensible experience; to build up, out of the distorted images of truth and beauty and nobility which the world presents to us, more perfect pictures of the same;—then imagination, so far from being an unimportant or superfluous element in our nature, is a faculty which is so nearly allied to reason that rational action would seem to be impossible apart from it. For this is the faculty which the scientific man uses when he forms his hypotheses and advances his science by means of them ; it is the faculty by which the novelist or philosopher builds up his ideals, and thereby gives impetus as well as aim to moral and political progress ; the faculty which the artist appeals to, when, through the medium of colour, or sound, or form, he presents to us the embodiment of ideas which their sensible materials can but suggest.

Or, descending to ordinary life, it is the faculty which enables men to break through the chains of ordinary commonplace routine, the oppressive dulness of a mere material life, and to come into contact with another order of things, whose capability of higher satisfaction and happiness comes home with a sense of infinite mystery and charm.

We must take human nature as we find it, and we have to face the fact that, in the lives of most men who rise at all above a mere animal existence, imagination, so far as we can treat it as a separate faculty, plays just as important a part as intellect ; that it indeed supplies most of the motive force and stimulating power which puts intellect itself into action, and bears no small share in the credit due to those achievements of the human mind which are generally looked upon as the special product of purely rational effort.

There is surely nothing irrational, then, in giving the due cultivation of this faculty a recognized place in that process of preparation which is to fit the mind for approaching a subject-matter which claims to be relative to all the capacities of human nature; to give them a full field for their development, a full and all-embracing object for their satisfaction.

One other characteristic I would mention, as naturally implied in the conception before us, and that is the characteristic of what we may call warm-heartedness, of sympathy and tender regard for our fellow-men. In a child's nature, the affections and sympathies are as a rule more active than they are in later life; it is as a rule more spontaneously affectionate, more loving, more responsive, and more dependent upon the display of similar feelings on the part of others. Such undoubtedly is a prominent attribute of a

childlike attitude of mind, and such is one
of the conditions of the right exercise of faith
implied by the reference to that attitude.
" How," the apostle asks, "can you love
God, Whom you have not seen, except you
love your fellow-men, whom you have seen ? "
How can you make that great act which
implies the exercise of the affections, no less
than that of the intellect, of the conscience,
and of the imagination, except you have
already trained those affections into organized activity by exercising them on the
appropriate objects which your relationships
with your fellow-men present ?

No exception is likely to be taken to such
a condition on the ground of irrationality,
since whatever criticism may be applied to
it would apply equally to those ties and
responsibilities and relationships which form

the very basis of our social system, and
a due recognition of which is one of the
requisites for the proper discharge of a man's
functions as a member of a family or a state.
But it is one thing to withhold a criticism
which could not be consistently maintained
without leading to disaster or absurdity;
another thing to practically ignore one of
the necessary conditions under which the
religious problem must be approached; to
treat that problem as if it were independent
of any preliminary conditions—as if its
solution could be as well attempted by those
who brought to its consideration no qualifi-
cations but such as can be attained in the
laboratory or in the dissecting-room, as by
those whose previous life and training were
such as would produce a sensitiveness to its
true significance, and a standard of reference

by which to judge of its claims to recognition and acknowledgment.

And this applies equally to all the conditions of faith which we have indicated above. Religion must be accepted on its own terms, or it cannot be accepted in any true sense of the word at all It is perfectly fair to criticize those terms, perfectly fair to subject them to the most careful scrutiny ; but until they are accepted, and until the mind has taken up the attitude which their acceptance implies, it is manifestly unfair to enter upon the discussion of facts which are relative to such an attitude, of experiences which can only be judged from its standpoint, of arguments and considerations which do not profess to carry conviction outside its range. Such a contention would at once be admitted with regard to any other department of thought or action. The scientist would treat with contempt the judgments of the unscientific world on his particular branch of knowledge ; the artist would be little affected by the criticisms of those whose artistic faculties were undeveloped and untrained ; the man of the world has little regard for the opinions of those who have had no practical experience of life. But an exception seems to be made when the religious subject-matter is approached. Here no special preliminary training seems to be thought necessary ; men whose whole life has been spent outside the range of those interests and influences and pursuits which more especially tend to produce the religious attitude of mind, have no hesitation in pronouncing judgment on religious questions, and in formulating theories to account for the growth and power of religious institutions; and, what is still more strange, their judgments and theories are deferred to by others, on the ground that they are more likely to be independent and free from bias.

True, such an exception is a tribute to the universality of the religious claim, and of the faculties to which it is relative; to the fact that all men are conscious of certain deep-felt wants which need a religious satisfaction. But this universality by no means dispenses with the necessity for the special training of those capacities — the due development and conscious recognition of those wants; and if these preliminary conditions have not been fulfilled, it is not religion's fault that the soul fails to find its due satisfaction. They form the threshold steps by which the Holy of holies is approached.

What wonder if those who try to enter the sanctuary without their aid find themselves baffled in the attempt!

Such are some, at any rate, of the more prominent conditions of faith, and there is nothing abnormal, nothing irrational in their requirements; nay, rather they represent but the developed form of principles which lie at the root of all social and personal progress. If, then, the charge of irrationality is to be maintained, its evidence must be looked for elsewhere.

V.

THE HYPOTHESIS OF FAITH.

THE conditions of faith having been fulfilled, certain capacities of heart and soul having been developed, a certain attitude of mind having been achieved, some of the leading characteristics of which have been indicated in the foregoing chapters, we come to the consideration of the next succeeding step in the progress of the soul towards its religious satisfaction.

Here it may be noticed that the succession we speak of is logical rather than actual, and represents the natural order in which the sequence of ideas arranges itself when reflected upon, rather than the historical form of that development in any particular case. This form will vary with circumstances and with the experiences of life, and in the normal case, as we may call it—the case of a man brought up from childhood in a Christian community, surrounded with Christian influences — the development of the activity of faith itself, and of the conditions on which that activity depends, may be simultaneous rather than successive. As the wants grow, they will be met with their due satisfaction ; as the capacities expand, they will find due field for their exercise ; as the sensibilities arise, they will find ready to hand the objects to which they are relative. The two will react on each other, and mutually define and inform each other.

But though very often, and under certain

circumstances generally, this is the actual course of the progress towards conscious faith, when that faith has become conscious, and the steps of the progress have been reflected upon, they will naturally divide themselves into a logical sequence, of which the first stage consists of preparation, of the development of a certain attitude of mind; the next, of active operation from the basis of that preparation, of the effort to attain an object of satisfaction clothed in the attributes which those conditions imply.

The first thing, then, is to see what those attributes are—the nature of the solution which a mind thus prepared would be disposed to accept as satisfactory.

First, take the condition of humility; of respect for authority, with the recognition of limitation of capacity; of weakness, both

G

of conception and endeavour, which that condition implies. This condition points at once towards some *external* source of satisfaction—points towards the fact that the object of faith cannot be self-evolved, but must be presented from without; must be derived from some objective source of power capable at once of supplying an embracing ideal of life, and of supplementing the recognized weakness of human nature by strength sufficient to make its attainment possible.

The second condition—that of moral integrity—will add something to our conception of the nature of this power; for it will point to the fact that it must be a moral power, a power from which can emanate nothing that can contradict the dictates of the conscience, or be inconsistent with them. Moreover, as these dictates present them-

selves as objective laws—laws holding good,
not only for the individual, but for all
rational beings—the source from which they
spring will naturally be identified with that
power outside us, which will thus come to
be looked upon as a *moral* power, a power
from which emanate moral ideals and the
strength necessary for their attainment ; and
therefore, since the ideals are of universal
application, and the strength relative to
universal and apparently well-nigh insuper-
able impediments, a power at once omnipotent and infinite in its range. Further still,
the moral law carries with it a sense not
only of fear, but of reverence and respect ;
and these are feelings which are not applicable to anything but a personal being.
Hence the external source of power becomes clothed, not merely with moral, but

also with personal attributes, *i.e.* with attributes of rational thought and self-conscious freedom ; and, by reasoning parallel to that which has gone before, a Personal Power, which is at once omnipotent and infinite, must be omniscient as well.

Such a conception once arrived at, the outline is very soon filled in ; attributes come crowding in from every quarter. The condition of spiritual sensitiveness which we have referred to will supply us with many rich details, with much vivid colouring ; will clothe the Personal Being with attributes of mystery, of majesty, of transcendent attractiveness and loveliness ; will turn our minds to it as the Source and final Consummation of all those broken glimpses of beauty which are brought to us through the medium of art, of poetry, of music, and of

philosophy. The fragments of ideal splen-
dour and glory which the imagination has
rescued from their environment of sense will
be brought thither for adjustment and ful-
filment; the vision of beauty which is looked
for must be one which will give them their
due place in its ordered symmetry.

Nor will the affections be content to be
left unsatisfied; they too will assert their
claim to recognition.

The personal Being, whose outline has
already been indicated, will not gain the
response of the whole nature unless He is
One round whom the heart's affections can
entwine themselves—One who will respond
to their advances, and will give them that
enduring solace and permanent fruition
which is denied to them in the transitory
scene of human society.

The capabilities which earthly relationships develop, only to disappoint, crave a
permanent outlet for their activity. The
object of satisfaction cannot be complete
which denies them this, which does not include the attributes of infinite and unchange-
able love, and tenderness, and sympathy,
and pity.

Moreover, it will be seen that such attributes imply something more. They imply
that the Being to whom they appertain
should be ready and willing to reveal Himself in the abundance of His soul-satisfying
power; and, since that Being is omnipotent, what He is willing to do He is able
to do, and the expectation is aroused that
such a revelation has been, or will in the
fulness of time be, vouchsafed.

The soul stands ready prepared, and the

crucial question, " Has it been ? " presents
itself with pressing urgency.   Hither and
thither it looks for an answer.   By this
hypothesis, and then by that, it endeavours
to meet the facts.   But vainly, till the eyes
turn to the face of the Crucified.   Here, and
here alone, it finds those attributes combined
which it seeks. *Objective authority* clear and
decisive : " Never man spake as this Man."
" He speaks with authority, and not as the
scribes ; " " I am the Way, the Truth, and the
Life." No mere dream of the imagination, no
mere self-originated ideal ; but a historical
Personage, the reality of whose life and
death and works of power is attested by the
clearest historical evidence. *Moral integrity*
fulfilling and transcending the highest conceptions of the most ideal speculation ; com-
bining in ordered harmony graces and virtues

which men only dreamt of before ; presenting a picture of perfection in which the most hostile criticism has been unable to find any flaw. " He did no sin," is the verdict which eighteen centuries of searching examination and controversy have unanimously returned ; here and here alone in the world's history we find a character whose spotless impeccability compels the reverence of even non-religious minds. *Forgiveness of sin ;* a way of escape held out from that web of delinquency and failure which seems to hold the soul bound to an irretrievable past, and to cast a shadow of despair over its future. " Thy sins be forgiven thee: rise up and walk "—words not lightly spoken, but the expression of a purpose and a power adequate to the tremendous issue involved ; a purpose which had been working itself out from the creation. and

which reached its consummation in the world
tragedy of Calvary; a power attested by
many outward signs of dominance over the
evil of the physical world, and finally placed
beyond dispute when, by the Resurrection,
death itself, the climax fact in which the
forces of moral and physical evil meet, was
overcome, and made the gate of everlasting
life. *Beauty* and *comeliness, spiritual grace*
and *mystery*, the story of Bethany and Nazareth, of Gethsemane and Calvary, contains
them all, from the softest and most delicate
notes of calm communion with God, to the
majestic terrors of a conflict in which the
spiritual forces of the universe met in a death-
struggle. They are all there ; the whole range
is touched ; everything that impresses the
imagination, that calls forth the hidden
activities of the spirit life in the soul, that

stimulates it to lift itself above the things of sense and time, and to unravel the secrets of its eternal destiny. For eighteen centuries an art and literature such as the world had never seen before have dealt with the material thus supplied, and still the source remains intact. It is a mine of riches as deep as eternity itself; the highest efforts of human genius are still but endeavours to bring to light some of the treasures it contains. *An object and source of sympathy and affection—* One who is touched with the feeling of our infirmities; who passed through all the relationships of social and domestic life; who spent anxious days and sleepless nights for our sakes; who showed in every action the warmest affection, the most sensitive regard; and who, by ascending into heaven with that very human body which was the vehicle and means of expression of these feelings, has assured us that the same ties of mutual endearment and response can bind us to Him which once united Him to His followers here on earth. The ascended Lord is still One to whom the weary and heavy laden can come, with the assurance of unfailing refreshment and relief. In Him all those instincts and impulses which are called forth by mutual intercourse and domestic life, can find the object on which alone they can concentrate without fear of disappointment or change; by union with Him can the expectations which these instincts produce, alone be realized to the full.

In thus indicating the steps of the process which we call *faith*, the process by which the soul passes from instinct to desire, from desire to expectation, and from expectation

to satisfaction and completion, it is hardly
necessary to say that neither the account
of the expectations aroused, nor of the attributes and characteristics of the great Object
to which they are relative, is intended to be
at all exhaustive. The human soul is infinite
in its capacities and aspirations; the Lord
of that soul has infinite means of satisfaction
and supply. Moreover, the points of first
attachment are equally various; the temple
of faith has many doors, and circumstances
and disposition determine that by which the
individual soul is led to enter. For one, the
door of intellect is easiest of approach; for
another, that of sympathy; for another, that
of spirit; but once inside, the life expands
to ever greater fulness of recognition and
expression, and the process is not complete
till every hidden energy has gained its true

outlet, every desire its appropriate satisfaction, every ideal its realization. The life
of faith is but another name for that eternal
development by which the soul grows up to
its full stature of conscious intercommunion
with the source of its being and the final
goal of its aspiration.

One of the main lines of that development,
as defined by the particular form of the
Christian revelation, we shall now endeavour
to indicate.

VI.

THE DEVELOPMENT OF FAITH.

THE essential and unique fact in the Christian revelation is the Incarnation. The other elements, as viewed in isolation from that fact, may be found elsewhere. Its *moral teaching*, e.g., is indeed unique, but only because it is summed up and concentrated in the life and work of a living Person ; because it is offered to us, not as an abstract system, but as a life-principle, translated into action under the pressure of the most trying and the most varied circumstances ; because the ideal presented to us is not a mere theory, but an actual and vivid realization under

conditions similar to those in which we ourselves are placed ; because the motive to
which it appeals is not mere reverence for
an impersonal law, but a spontaneous response of personal devotion, which combines
the forces of affection and imagination with
those of conscientious adhesion to moral
right ; because, above all, it holds out a way
of escape from the deadening effects of past
sin and inherited tendency, and opens up a
source from which power may be derived to
meet its demands. But take away from it
these elements, all of which are directly
dependent on the fact of the Incarnation,
look at it merely as a series of detached
moral precepts, and there is nothing in it
which gives it a claim to pre-eminence. Nay,
more ; the essential principle of its unity
being thus withdrawn, it becomes incoherent,

and to a large extent unintelligible. That delicate gradation of appeals ranging from the most elementary forms of prudential self-interest to the highest flights of self-sacrificing love, so well adapted to the varying stages of moral and spiritual sensibility on the part of Christ's hearers, would, when translated into the language of mere formal ethics, and deprived of the key which harmonizes them into an intelligible whole, become but a heterogeneous series of disconnected statements, not to be classified under any single moral theory. The moral philosophy of Christianity is the Incarnate Christ ; take Him away, His life, His death, His historical reality, and instead of a philosophy we have but a collection of discordant aphorisms. And what is true of the moral teaching of Christianity is equally true of its *spiritual revelation*. The domain of the spiritual life was not a new region opened up by Christianity. Before Christ's advent men had gained entrance there ; had tasted something of the sweetness of communion with the Divine Source of their being ; had gained some knowledge of the means by which their spiritual faculties could be developed and quickened ; had formulated those means into a definite science of devotion ; had in some instances made such progress that the language in which their spiritual experiences are outpoured has become the mother tongue of the devotional life. In the language of the psalms, for instance, the Church still finds the natural expression of her worship, the fitting training-ground of her saints. But she only does so because into that language she reads the facts from which her own life

H

springs. The spiritual life to Plato, to the Bhuddist sages, to the Old Testament saints, was at best a cloudland region, full of mysterious forms and changing shapes—a region of conjecture and speculation and uncertainty. The Divine Presence they knew to be there, but a wall of thick darkness shrouded it from them, and only by intermittent rays could they see its glory reflected in the symbols and types of the world of sense. It was this wall that the Incarnation broke down. The Light of the world is no reflection, but the primal source of all light; a sustained consistent advance in the knowledge of spiritual things has become possible because a definite Object has been presented on which the mind can concentrate, and that an Object in which all the energies of heart and soul and spirit can

find their full response and their possibility
of complete development.

The spiritual life is but another name for
conscious communion with the Incarnate
Christ. Take away the Incarnation, and it
becomes but an unsatisfied longing ; but a
vague experiment in the regions of boundless
mystery.

The same considerations apply to all the
other peculiar features of the Christian revelation. Its response to the affections and
sympathies depends on the fact that it places
before us One who, by personal experience
of the conditions of human life, became
touched with the feelings of our infirmities ;
its offer of pardon and reconciliation would
bear with it no credentials of its adequacy
and authenticity, were it not for the life-
struggle which culminated in Calvary and

the guarantee of its triumph in the Resurrection. And so it is all along the line; the Incarnation is the corner-stone of the Christian edifice; take it away, and the whole fabric dissolves into ruin.

Whether these results could have been achieved by any other means, whether a revelation adequate to human need could have been made in any other way, is beside the point; for the Christian it is sufficient to know that this is the form which God's revelation of Himself has taken, and that it meets all the necessities of the case.

Here, then, is a fundamental fact which must be accepted as a guiding principle by all who have made the Christian hypothesis of faith, and which must direct their efforts as they proceed to develop that hypothesis, by including under it all the experiences and claims of life—a fact fruitful in implications of great practical importance.

One such implication I would touch briefly upon ; one of the main lines along which it extends itself to the life of the individual and the community.

If we examine the Incarnation as God's method of revealing His nature to us, we shall find, I think, that among its chief characteristics are the following :—

1. It is an *external* revelation ; it takes up the elements of sense into the divine life, and makes them its vehicle of expression and means of application.

2. It is a revelation under a *definite* external form. It is not merely that nature as a whole was consecrated to divine uses, but one particular form of natural life was selected for this purpose, and made the connecting link

between the natural and the supernatural ; the gate through which the supernatural could flow into the natural world, and absorb it into itself.

3. The external form thus selected was the form of *man*.

4. Man is the centre of a twofold system of relationships. He is Nature's highest product, summing up all Nature's powers, and being in turn himself dependent on them for sustenance and support. He is, moreover, connected with his fellow-men by such intimate ties, that in isolation he would be a mere vague potentiality, his capacities undeveloped, his life without a content. This twofold order—the order of nature and the order of society—Christ, by taking on Him the form of man, united in Himself; they contributed to the maintenance and

expression of the divine life under that form, and were thus consecrated as the means of God's revelation therein contained. Not the order of nature in general, or of society in general, but particular portions of these which were brought into relationship with the life of the Incarnate Christ: the particular food which He ate; the particular drink which He drank; the particular men who surrounded Him and who formed His social environment; all nature and all humanity, indeed, were thus potentially affected, but only because certain definite portions of each were selected and set apart as the instruments of a life which could through their means permeate through the orders of being to which they belonged.

Such are some of the characteristics of the Incarnation viewed as the *means* through

which God has revealed Himself to man;
and if we examine those characteristics we
shall find nothing in them which would seem
to limit them to one particular stage of the
world's history, but much that would lead
us to expect that they should be made a
continuous element in that history; that the
Incarnation was the starting-point of a new
order of life rather than an isolated fact in
the world's progress. In one sense, indeed,
the Incarnation does stand alone; it was
the concentrating of the whole nature of God
in the life and work of an individual Man-
hood, and, from the nature of the case, that
must form a climax of revelation such as can
never be reached again.

But when we consider its application to
men, its gradual development in the life of
humanity as a practical principle and a

guiding power, all the wants to which these characteristics were relative still assert themselves as permanent elements in human nature, and still claim their satisfaction.

The *historical character* of the revelation, for instance, the fact that it was clothed in an external form and appealed to us through our external senses, met the deep-seated craving of the human mind for an objective source of religious authority and power, one which would be independent of the passing phases of individual thought and feeling, and remain constant and unalterable, however much they varied.

The *definiteness* of that external form added an element of simplicity and security to that satisfaction—made the source of religious power more easy of access and application.   It was not merely the voice of God

speaking through the general order of nature
that we were called to hear ; this voice might
be hard to hear at times, and difficult of
interpretation ; but it was His message concentrated in its fulness in the living action
of one particular form of natural product.
The exigencies of practical life demand a
definite authoritative guidance, if we are to
meet them promptly and resolutely ; that
guidance was within the reach of those who
followed the footsteps of the Incarnate
Christ, and heard the utterances of His living
voice—utterances which were concerned, not
merely with general principles of conduct,
but which dealt with the detail difficulties
of ordinary commonplace existence as well,
and solved them by placing them in the
context of a higher order of reality.

But is such guidance unnecessary now ?

Is not human nature still the same? Are not men still liable to be confused and carried away by circumstance? Do they not still need an external Source of power which will reinforce their inner tendency to good, by something more than theoretical conviction ; which will combine the broken fragments of their higher hopes and aspirations and inclinations in the unity of an ordered system of life, and bestow on them at once a field of action, a source of power, and a definite object of attainment?

Again, the external form was that of a *Man*, and in that fact was summed up the satisfaction of all those wants which men try to satisfy by human companionship and sympathy and society ; all those ever-changing needs and necessities which can only be met by the response of living personality. It was in living contact with the personal Christ that men found what their souls desired, and that contact implied, as its necessary ground and means of expression, a social relationship of a definite external kind, a relationship which included not merely the individual and Christ, but all those other individuals who surrounded Him, and the world of natural phenomena, which both contributed to His material maintenance and furnished the field of His physical activity.

But here, again, we come upon a system of wants of permanent character. Man still is dependent on society and on nature for the development of his capacities and for their maintenance; and if the Incarnation consecrated that dependence for those who were contemporaries of Christ, by making the link which binds us to our fellow-men and the world in which we live the same which unites us to the Source of all life, there is no reason which, so far as we can see, would lead us to suppose that this channel of divine Power should have been closed on the day of the Ascension ; rather should we expect that it would be made a permanent means of grace, that the Word made flesh would continue to be the pattern of the divine method.

Thus we see that for any one who accepts the Incarnate Christ as the working hypothesis of his religious life, as the ultimate solution of his intellectual difficulties and the ultimate satisfaction of his moral aspirations, that acceptance, when reflected upon, is at once found to be fruitful in implications transcending the range of any past historical fact ; for such a fact would at best but substitute a memory for a hope ; but leading him to expect that the Incarnation, in all its essential characteristics, has become a permanent and potent factor in the progress of the world ; that the Fountain Source of religious life is still an external objective source of a definite, clearly marked form ; and that it still uses as its medium and means of expression both the relationships of human society and the products of material nature.

How far such expectations are the legitimate offspring of his primary act of faith, can only be judged by looking at them in the light of the facts of Christ's own teaching, of the facts of the historical development of Christianity, and of the facts of the experience of those who for the last eighteen hundred years have made Christianity their working principle of life. Turning to these facts, then, what do we find ? We find in them the amplest justification, the most abundant and most definite response ; for they all concur in affirming that the visible manifestation of the highest form of life did not end on the day of the Ascension ; that it still remains among us, and still in an Incarnate form; in the form of a human organization instead of a human organism ; that the Church is the body of Christ, and possesses the attributes and discharges the functions which His human body once did ; with a definite place in history, with a definite external form, just as His human body had, with definite organs, with definite means of expression; the medium through which He still reveals Himself to man, through which He still acts upon their souls, through which He still unites them to Himself, through which He still bestows on them the strength they need. Nor is the world of nature apart from man left outside the range of the divine order thus established. Nature's contribution to Christ's body is still maintained. As the food which He ate and the drink which He drank, when assimilated by the processes peculiar to His human body, became part of that body itself, and thus became the means of expressing and sustaining the divine life of which that body was the clothing; so still the primary elements of natural produce, when assimilated by the processes peculiar to His Body the Church, become incorporated with that Body itself, and form the means of its sustenance and support.

So the doctrine of the Incarnation, when reflected upon, is seen to imply as its corollary and its necessary sequel the doctrine of the Church and of the sacraments; and once that level has been attained, the way seems clear which leads man forward to his eternal destiny. He no longer depends on his own unaided intellect as the guide to speculative and practical truth. He willingly corrects its conclusions by those which the united Christian consciousness has, under the guidance of the indwelling Spirit, deduced from the experiences of eighteen hundred years; willingly recognizes in the authoritative decisions of the Church the voice of Christ Himself, speaking through the appropriate organs of His Body. He no longer needs to seek a fitting outlet for the energies of his life, a fitting ideal towards which to strive ; he finds himself brought into imme- diate relationship with a great system of organized effort and devotion, which leaves no part of his life outside its activity, but claims

I

his whole nature as an instrument for its development. It is as a member of the Body that he takes his place in the world, and his whole activity is absorbed in discharging duly the responsibilities of that membership.

Nor is that activity any longer neutralized by the knowledge of inherent weakness, and the haunting heritage of past sin and failure. The society with which he has identified himself reinforces his weakness by its own divine strength, and rescues him from his past by its own proper remedies. Through definite external channels, through means whose validity in no wise depends upon the passing phases of personal feeling, it brings to him its life-giving powers, and declares to him its authoritative message of absolution. His nature, with all its wants and capacities, with all its aspirations and ideals, with all its sympathies and affections and desires, here attains its highest level. It here passes into its final stage of development—a development infinite in its possibilities, eternal in its manifestation, for its climax is the Incarnate God Himself. Here, in that unbroken line of organized corporate life which history presents to us, descending like a stream of limpid waters from the Source of all life ; fertilizing the desert places through which it passes ; making the wastes of human passion and brutality to blossom with the sweet flowers of civilization ; inviting us by the very music of its movement to take of its living waters, and in their strength to do our God-appointed work, and then, with the souls whom we have helped to save, to embark upon its kindly bosom, and there be borne in safety to that ocean of eternal rest on which the Sun of Righteousness never sets.

VII.

CONCLUSION.

WE have tried to trace the steps of the
process by which an individual soul arrives
at that great spiritual attainment which we
call faith, and by which, further, it develops
that attainment into its full expression in the
creeds and system of the Catholic Church ;
and we have tried to show that none of these
steps are irrational or out of analogy with the
action of the mind in other departments of
knowledge and belief, whose validity would
not be called into account except by those
who denied the possibility of any knowledge.

In doing this we have concentrated our
attention almost altogether on the action of

the mind itself, beginning with its wants and capacities, and going on to its action in satisfying those wants and realizing those capacities; and we have assumed that such satisfaction, when completely attained by ourselves and by others, is the only possible proof of truth and the only possible guarantee of validity. Such an assumption, however, is likely to be criticized from two different points of view.

In the first place, many religious minds will reject the description of faith based upon it as inadequate. The faith of which they are conscious, they will say, is more than the satisfaction of purely human wants, is more than a hypothesis justifying itself by its results; it is a transcendental fact, a gift from the outside, which carries its own justification with it. The wants which it satisfies are not merely those of the natural man, but others which are engrafted on our nature by the same Power which satisfies them. Not merely is the object of faith a gift of the Spirit, but the capacity to receive it is such as well.

But that this is so may be admitted without allowing the criticism founded upon it to be applicable here. For all we have endeavoured to show is that, so far as faith arises from recognized conditions, and so far as its action is of an ostensible character, it follows rational laws and is capable of rational justification, and that therefore the believing Christian need not be afraid to submit his religious belief to the most searching examination, nor need he fear that it cannot be shown to stand on the same level of intellectual validity as his other beliefs. The further sanction of faith, the divine action which, in some cases at any rate, lifts it at once from the level of gradually converging probability to that of transcendental certainty, does not come within our range of consideration.

Two suggestions may, however, be made with regard to it.

Firstly, there are reasons for supposing that this transcendental conviction often varies in strength in inverse proportion to the capacity for mental analysis and rational endeavour. The conscious "assurance" of the truth of his belief is often more intensely realized by the converted peasant than by the educated Christian ; and, if this be so, it would seem to point to the conclusion that God in His mercy supplies the deficiencies of His weaker children by special gifts of His grace, and enables them by their means to overcome the haunting sense of insecurity as to the foundations of their belief, otherwise sure to arise were those foundations challenged by arguments and statements above the standard of their intellectual capacities. But from those whom He has endowed with greater powers, He demands an exercise of them proportionate to their endowment, and calls them to consecrate them to His service, through the endeavour to bring all truth into conscious relation with the foundation Truth of their spiritual life.

Secondly, the distinction between natural and supernatural wants is difficult of application in the case of those whose nature has been regenerated by the waters of holy baptism. The supernatural for them has become, potentially at any rate, the natural ; and it does not require the assumption of the creation of new spiritual wants to account for their response to the object of faith, since such wants lie dormant in the baptismal germ of life, and only need the normal influences of a Christian society to develop them into conscious activity.

The second criticism to which we have referred is based on different grounds. Our assumption itself may be assailed as intellectually untenable ; as providing no adequate safeguard against a false and dangerous system of *a priori* reasoning, which would tend to lead those who committed themselves to it to fantastic and unreal results ; which has, indeed, before now produced such results, and by their means clouded the human intellect and impeded its healthy development.

The reverse method, it may be argued, has been proved to be the true one. If we are to arrive at the truth of things, we must not begin with our own self-formed theories, and endeavour to make facts fit into them ; we must begin with the facts of experience, and gradually let our theory grow out of them. Then, and then only, can we be assured that our theories hold good in the realm of objective reality, and are not mere dreams of our own imagination.

The exhaustive consideration of the questions suggested by this criticism would, we need hardly say, involve the discussion of the most difficult and subtle problems of metaphysical science. It would be necessary for us, for instance, before we approached them, to define what a fact was, what we meant by objective reality, how that reality is subjectively apprehended, and what are the relations between subject and object in the process.

Such problems, however, lie altogether

outside the limits of our discussion. We have,
as we have said, endeavoured to begin where
metaphysics leaves off; that is to say, we
have endeavoured to take human belief and
thought as we find them, and endeavoured
to see whether the conditions and considerations which lead to religious faith are in
analogy with those which are generally
admitted as valid in other departments of
rational action. The metaphysical explana-
tion of the processes on which those conditions and considerations depend does not
come within the scope of our inquiry, since it
would apply equally to all classes of thought,
and would have a similar bearing on the
secular and religious domain.

One tentative remark, however, may be
ventured with regard to this question. It is
well for us to remember that to begin with

facts is not to begin outside the province of the mind's action. Facts become so for us only when they enter into experience, that is, when they are related by the mind's action to other facts similarly conditioned. A fact, indeed, so far as we can have cognizance of it, is but a synthesis of such relations, and is therefore implicitly the basis of a theory, since a theory is only another name for the explicit recognition of a system of relations holding good between a number of facts. In other words, in the very act of apprehending a fact we instinctively form a theory about it, or what we have called a hypothesis ; and the truth of the apprehension depends upon the truth of that hypothesis, which in the last resort is assured to us by an act of self-recognition, by the mind's acceptance of it as its own product—a development of itself, embodying its own laws and carrying out its own principles.

What is called *a priori* reasoning, then, does not seem to differ in kind from any other sort of reasoning. All reasoning is, in a sense, *a priori;* and when it leads to inadequate results, it is not because of its *a priori* character, not because the mind proceeds from itself and returns to itself again, but because this self is an undeveloped self—one which is not fully conscious of its own content; which has not fully recognized what its capacities are, what its powers of growth; and which therefore, outside a limited range, is not in a position to judge of the adequacy of any theory, or of its relation to the whole range of mental and moral experience.

The conclusions based on such reasoning are dangerous when, on the mind becoming conscious of a new order of experiences, or on its attention being concentrated on them for the first time, it does not recognize them as new, but, assuming them to be of a like character to those with which it has hitherto been conversant, proceeds to force them into its previous theories, whether they will or no, explaining away or disregarding altogether those for which it cannot find a place.

A priori reasoning, in this sense of the word, has undoubtedly been the fruitful parent of error and confusion; the old bottles have proved but sorry receptacles for the new wine which it was attempted to make them hold. But it can hardly be alleged with fairness that such attempts have been the monopoly of religious apologists. Indeed, it is not overstating the case to say that the most pronounced exponents of this

narrow and one-sided method have of late
years, at any rate, been found among the
leaders of materialistic and so-called ra-
tionalistic speculation—men whose attention,
having been concentrated on the physical
laws of the universe, and on the attempt to
unravel nature's secrets by their means, have
come to regard the facts which they investigate as the only facts worth investigating,
and the laws which they see hold good in
them—the mere surface laws by which they
classify and generalize them—to be the only
laws worthy of the name ; and who, when
we bring before their notice the experiences
of the spiritual consciousness, either reject
them at once with scorn as unreal hallu-
cinations, or attempt to explain them by
explaining them away—by resolving them
into their physical conditions, and making

them subject to the laws which govern those conditions.

It is against this false *a priori* method, this narrow and one-sided rationalism, that the Church raises her principal protest at the present day. The religion of the Incarnation includes all human powers and capacities within its range. It only insists that they should all be included ; that the *whole* nature of man should be made its test and standard of reference, not disjointed fragments or partial developments of that nature. Above all, it insists that man's spiritual capacities— that part of his nature through which he comes into direct personal communion with God—should be developed in proportion to his other capacities ; that they should not be starved and deadened by neglect, while his energies are absorbed in intellectual interests or practical pursuits; that his habits of devotion, of aspiration, of prayer, of meditation, should be trained and cultivated as much as those of mental dexterity or worldly prudence; that, in other words, before we put faith to the test of logical analysis, we should first establish the mental, moral, and spiritual conditions which it demands, and from which alone it can spring.

The demand is surely not an unreasonable one. Christianity claims to regenerate the whole man, and it is to the whole man that its appeal is made. Nor can it be justly said to have proved inadequate if that appeal is not responded to by those who have deliberately closed the channel through which its voice can first be most readily heard.

PRINTED BY WILLIAM CLOWES AND SONS, LIMITED,
LONDON AND BECCLES.

K

39 PATERNOSTER ROW, LONDON, E.C.
February 1893.

A Catalogue of Works

IN

THEOLOGICAL LITERATURE

PUBLISHED BY

MESSRS. LONGMANS, GREEN, & CO.

MESSRS. LONGMANS, GREEN, & CO.

Issue the undermentioned Lists of their Publications, which may be had post free on application:—

1. MONTHLY LIST OF NEW WORKS AND NEW EDITIONS.

2. QUARTERLY LIST OF ANNOUNCEMENTS AND NEW WORKS.

3. NOTES ON BOOKS: BEING AN ANALYSIS OF THE WORKS PUBLISHED DURING EACH QUARTER.

4. CATALOGUE OF SCIENTIFIC WORKS.

5. CATALOGUE OF MEDICAL AND SURGICAL WORKS.

6. CATALOGUE OF SCHOOL BOOKS AND EDUCATIONAL WORKS.

7. CATALOGUE OF BOOKS FOR ELEMENTARY SCHOOLS AND PUPIL TEACHERS.

8. CATALOGUE OF WORKS IN THEOLOGICAL LITERATURE.

9. CATALOGUE OF WORKS IN GENERAL LITERATURE.

Abbey and Overton.—THE ENGLISH CHURCH IN THE EIGHTEENTH CENTURY. By CHARLES J. ABBEY, M.A., Rector of Checkendon, Reading, and JOHN H. OVERTON, M.A., Canon of Lincoln, Rector of Epworth, Doncaster. *Crown 8vo. 7s. 6d.*

Adams.—SACRED ALLEGORIES. The Shadow of the Cross —The Distant Hills—The Old Man's Home—The King's Messengers. By the Rev. WILLIAM ADAMS, M.A., late Fellow of Merton College, Oxford. *Crown 8vo. 3s. 6d.*

The Four Allegories may be had separately, with Illustrations 16mo. 1s. each.

Aids to the Inner Life.

Edited by the Rev. W. H. HUTCHINGS, M.A., Rector of Kirkby
Misperton, Yorkshire. *Five Vols. 32mo, cloth limp, 6d. each ; or cloth
extra, 1s. each. Sold separately.*

Also an Edition *with red borders,* 2s. each.

OF THE IMITATION OF CHRIST. By THOMAS À KEMPIS. In
Four Books.

THE CHRISTIAN YEAR. Thoughts in Verse for the Sundays and
Holy Days throughout the Year.

THE DEVOUT LIFE. By ST. FRANCIS DE SALES.

THE HIDDEN LIFE OF THE SOUL. From the French of JEAN
NICHOLAS GROU.

THE SPIRITUAL COMBAT. Together with the Supplement and the
Path of Paradise. By LAURENCE SCUPOLI.

Alford.—Works by HENRY ALFORD, D.D., late Dean of Canterbury.

THE GREEK TESTAMENT, with a critically Revised Text ; a Digest
of Various Readings ; Marginal References to Verbal and Idiomatic
Usage ; Prolegomena ; and a Critical and Exegetical Commentary.
For the use of Theological Students and Ministers. *Four Vols. 8vo.
102s. Sold separately.*

Vol. I.—THE FOUR GOSPELS. 28s.

Vol. II.—ACTS TO II. CORINTHIANS. 24s.

Vol. III.—GALATIANS TO PHILEMON. 18s.

Vol. IV.—HEBREWS TO REVELATION. 32s.

THE NEW TESTAMENT FOR ENGLISH READERS : containing
the Authorised Version, with a Revised English Text, Marginal
References, and a Critical and Explanatory Commentary. *Two Vols.
4 Parts. 8vo. 54s. 6d. Sold separately.*

Vol. I., Part 1—THE FIRST THREE GOSPELS. 12s.

Vol. I., Part 2—ST. JOHN AND THE ACTS. 10s. 6d.

Vol. II., Part 1—THE EPISTLES OF ST. PAUL. 16s.

Vol. II., Part 2—HEBREWS TO REVELATION. 16s.

SERMONS FOR THE CHRISTIAN YEAR. A Selection from the
Quebec Chapel Sermons.

Vol. I.—ADVENT TO TRINITY. *Crown 8vo.* 6s.

Vol. II.—TRINITY TO ALL SAINTS' DAY. *Crown 8vo.* 5s.

Allen.—THE CHURCH CATECHISM : its History and
Contents. A Manual for Teachers and Students. By the Rev.
A. J. C. ALLEN, M.A., Vicar of St. Mary-the-Less, Cambridge,
formerly Principal of the Chester Diocesan Training College. *Crown
8vo.* 3s. 6d.

Andrewes.—A MANUAL FOR THE SICK ; with other Devotions. By LANCELOT ANDREWES, D.D., sometime Bishop of Winchester. Edited, with a Preface, by H. P. LIDDON, D.D., late Chancellor and Canon of St. Paul's. *With Portrait.* 24mo. 2s. 6d.

Arnold.—SERMONS PREACHED MOSTLY IN THE CHAPEL OF RUGBY SCHOOL. By THOMAS ARNOLD, D.D., formerly Head Master of Rugby School. *Six Vols. Crown 8vo,* 30s.; *or separately,* 5s. *each.*

Augustine.—THE CONFESSIONS OF ST. AUGUSTINE. In Ten Books. Translated and Edited by the Rev. W. H. HUTCHINGS, M.A., Rector of Kirkby Misperton, Yorkshire. *Small 8vo.* 5s. *Cheap Edition.* 16mo. 2s. 6d.

Ayre.—THE TREASURY OF BIBLE KNOWLEDGE : being a Dictionary of the Books, Persons, Places, Events, and other matters of which mention is made in Holy Scripture. By the Rev. J. AYRE, M.A. With 5 Maps, 15 Plates, and 300 Woodcuts. *Fcap. 8vo.* 6s.

Baker.—Works by the Rev. WILLIAM BAKER, D.D., Head Master of Merchant Taylors' School, and Prebendary of St. Paul's.

A MANUAL OF DEVOTION FOR SCHOOLBOYS. With Preface by J. R. WOODFORD, D.D., late Bishop of Ely. *Crown 16mo, cloth limp.* 1s. 6d.

DAILY PRAYERS FOR YOUNGER BOYS. 32mo. 8d.

A PLAIN EXPOSITION OF THE THIRTY-NINE ARTICLES OF THE CHURCH OF ENGLAND, for the use of Schools. 16mo. 2s. 6d.

Ball.—THE REFORMED CHURCH OF IRELAND, 1537-1889. By the Right Hon. J. T. BALL, LL.D., D.C.L. *8vo.* 7s. 6d.

Baring-Gould.—THE ORIGIN AND DEVELOPMENT OF RELIGIOUS BELIEF. By the Rev. S. BARING-GOULD, M.A. *Two Parts. Crown 8vo.* 3s. 6d. *each.*

Part I.—MONOTHEISM AND POLYTHEISM.
Part II.—CHRISTIANITY.

Barry.—SOME LIGHTS OF SCIENCE ON THE FAITH. Being the Bampton Lectures for 1892. By the Right Rev. ALFRED BARRY, D.D., Canon of Windsor, formerly Bishop of Sydney, Metropolitan of New South Wales, and Primate of Australia. *8vo.* 12s. 6d.

Bathe.—Works by the Rev. ANTHONY BATHE, M.A.

AN ADVENT WITH JESUS. 32*mo*, 1*s.*; *or in paper cover*, 6*d.*

A LENT WITH JESUS. A Plain Guide for Churchmen. Containing Readings for Lent and Easter Week, and on the Holy Eucharist. 32*mo*, 1*s.*; *or in paper cover*, 6*d.*

WHAT I SHOULD BELIEVE. A Simple Manual of Self-Instruction for Church People. *Crown 8vo.* 3*s.* 6*d.*

Benson.—THE FINAL PASSOVER : A Series of Meditations upon the Passion of our Lord Jesus Christ. By the Rev. R. M. BENSON, M.A., Student of Christ Church, Oxford. Vol. 3. THE DIVINE EXODUS—Parts I. and II.

Bickersteth.—YESTERDAY, TO-DAY, AND FOR EVER : a Poem in Twelve Books. By EDWARD HENRY BICKERSTETH, D.D., Bishop of Exeter. *One Shilling Edition*, 18*mo.* *With red borders*, 16*mo*, 2*s.* 6*d.*

The Crown 8vo Edition (5*s.*) *may still be had.*

Birch.—THE SACRAMENT OF THE LORD'S SUPPER, ACCORDING TO THE TEACHING OF THE PRIMITIVE CHURCH AND OF ANGLICAN DIVINES. By EDWARD JONATHAN BIRCH, M.A., Rector of Overstone and Hon. Canon of Peterborough. 18*mo.* 1*s.*

Blore.—THE WEIGHTY CHARGE : a Series of Addresses to Ordination Candidates. By Rev. GEORGE J. BLORE, D.D., formerly Head Master of King's School, Canterbury. *Crown 8vo.* 3*s.* 6*d.*

Blunt.—Works by the Rev. JOHN HENRY BLUNT, D.D.

THE ANNOTATED BOOK OF COMMON PRAYER: Being an Historical, Ritual, and Theological Commentary on the Devotional System of the Church of England. Edited by the Rev. JOHN HENRY BLUNT, D.D. 4*to.* 21*s.*

THE COMPENDIOUS EDITION OF THE ANNOTATED BOOK OF COMMON PRAYER: Forming a concise Commentary on the Devotional System of the Church of England. Edited by the Rev. JOHN HENRY BLUNT, D.D. *Crown 8vo.* 10*s.* 6*d.*

DICTIONARY OF DOCTRINAL AND HISTORICAL THEOLOGY. By various Writers. Edited by the Rev. JOHN HENRY BLUNT, D.D. *Imperial 8vo.* 21*s.*

DICTIONARY OF SECTS, HERESIES, ECCLESIASTICAL PARTIES AND SCHOOLS OF RELIGIOUS THOUGHT. By various Writers. Edited by the Rev. JOHN HENRY BLUNT, D.D. *Imperial 8vo.* 21*s.*

[*continued.*

Blunt.—Works by the Rev. JOHN HENRY BLUNT, D.D.—*contd.*

THE REFORMATION OF THE CHURCH OF ENGLAND: its History, Principles, and Results. *Two Vols. 8vo. Sold separately.*

> Vol. I.—A.D. 1514-1547. Its Progress during the reign of Henry VIII. 16*s.*

> Vol. II.—A.D. 1547-1662. From the death of Henry VIII. to the Restoration of the Church after the Commonwealth. 18*s.*

THE BOOK OF CHURCH LAW. Being an Exposition of the Legal Rights and Duties of the Parochial Clergy and the Laity of the Church of England. Revised by Sir WALTER G. F. PHILLIMORE, Bart., D.C.L. *Crown 8vo. 7s. 6d.*

DIRECTORIUM PASTORALE. The Principles and Practice of Pastoral Work in the Church of England. *Crown 8vo. 7s. 6d.*

A COMPANION TO THE BIBLE: Being a Plain Commentary on Scripture History, to the end of the Apostolic Age. *Two vols. small 8vo. Sold separately.*

> THE OLD TESTAMENT. 3*s.* 6*d.*   THE NEW TESTAMENT. 3*s.* 6*d.*

HOUSEHOLD THEOLOGY: a Handbook of Religious Information respecting the Holy Bible, the Prayer Book, the Church, the Ministry, Divine Worship, the Creeds, etc. etc. *Paper cover, 16mo.* 1*s.* *Also the Larger Edition,* 3*s.* 6*d.*

Body.—Works by the Rev. GEORGE BODY, D.D., Canon Missioner of the Diocese of Durham.

THE LIFE OF LOVE. A Course of Lent Lectures. *Crown 8vo.* 4*s.* 6*d.*

THE SCHOOL OF CALVARY ; or, Laws of Christian Life revealed from the Cross. A Course of Lectures delivered in substance at All Saints', Margaret Street. *Small 8vo.* 3*s.* 6*d.*

THE LIFE OF JUSTIFICATION: a Series of Lectures delivered in substance at All Saints', Margaret Street. *16mo.* 2*s.* 6*d.*

THE LIFE OF TEMPTATION: a Course of Lectures delivered in substance at St. Peter's, Eaton Square; also at all Saints' Margaret Street. *16mo.* 2*s.* 6*d.*

Bonaventure.—THE LIFE OF CHRIST. By ST. BONAVENTURE. Translated and Edited by the Rev. W. H. HUTCHINGS, M.A., Rector of Kirkby Misperton, Yorkshire. *Crown 8vo.* 7*s.* 6*d.*

Bonney.—CHRISTIAN DOCTRINES AND MODERN THOUGHT: being the Boyle Lectures for 1891. By the Rev. T. G. BONNEY, D.Sc., LL.D., Hon. Canon of Manchester. *Crown 8vo.* 5*s.*

Boultbee.—A COMMENTARY ON THE THIRTY-NINE ARTICLES OF THE CHURCH OF ENGLAND. By the Rev. T. P. BOULTBEE, formerly Principal of the London College of Divinity, St. John's Hall, Highbury. *Crown 8vo. 6s.*

Bright.—Works by WILLIAM BRIGHT, D.D., Canon of Christ Church, and Regius Professor of Ecclesiastical History in the University of Oxford.
MORALITY IN DOCTRINE. *Crown 8vo. 7s. 6d.*
LESSONS FROM THE LIVES OF THREE GREAT FATHERS: St. Athanasius, St. Chrysostom, and St. Augustine. With Appendices. *Crown 8vo. 6s.*
THE INCARNATION AS A MOTIVE POWER. *Crown 8vo. 6s.*

Bright and Medd.—LIBER PRECUM PUBLICARUM EC- CLESIÆ ANGLICANÆ. A GULIELMO BRIGHT, S.T.P., Ædis Christi apud Oxon. Canonico, Historiæ Ecclesiasticæ, Professore Regio, et PETRO GOLDSMITH MEDD, A.M., Eccles. Cath. S. Albani Canonico Honorario, Collegii Universitatis apud Oxon. Socio Seniore. Latine redditus. [In hac Editione continentur Versiones Latinæ— 1. Libri Precum Publicarum Ecclesiæ Anglicanæ ; 2. Liturgiæ Primæ Reformatæ ; 3. Liturgiæ Scoticanæ ; 4. Liturgiæ Americanæ.] *Editio Quarta*, cum Appendice. *With Rubrics in red. Small 8vo. 7s. 6d.*

Browne.—AN EXPOSITION OF THE THIRTY-NINE ARTICLES, Historical and Doctrinal. By E. H. BROWNE, D.D., formerly Bishop of Winchester. *8vo. 16s.*

Campion and Beamont.—THE PRAYER BOOK INTER- LEAVED. With Historical Illustrations and Explanatory Notes arranged parallel to the Text. By W. M. CAMPION, D.D., and W. J. BEAMONT, M.A. *Small 8vo. 7s. 6d.*

Carter.—PREPARATION FOR WORSHIP. A Series of Five Short Addresses on the Last Answer in the Church Catechism. By F. E. CARTER, M.A., Canon Missioner of Truro Cathedral. *Small 8vo. 2s.*

Carter.—Works edited by the Rev. T. T. CARTER, M.A., Hon. Canon of Christ Church, Oxford.
THE TREASURY OF DEVOTION : a Manual of Prayer for General and Daily Use. Compiled by a Priest. *18mo. 2s. 6d. ; cloth limp*, *2s. ; or bound with the Book of Common Prayer, 3s. 6d. Large-Type Edition. Crown 8vo. 3s. 6d.*

[continued.

Carter.—Works edited by the Rev. T. T. CARTER, M.A., Hon. Canon of Christ Church, Oxford—*continued.*

THE WAY OF LIFE: A Book of Prayers and Instruction for the Young at School, with a Preparation for Confirmation. Compiled by a Priest. 18mo. 1s. 6d.

THE PATH OF HOLINESS: a First Book of Prayers, with the Service of the Holy Communion, for the Young. Compiled by a Priest. With Illustrations. 16mo. 1s. 6d. ; *cloth limp*, 1s.

THE GUIDE TO HEAVEN : a Book of Prayers for every Want. (For the Working Classes.) Compiled by a Priest. 18mo. 1s. 6d. ; *cloth limp*, 1s. *Large-Type Edition. Crown 8vo. 1s. 6d. ; cloth limp*, 1s.

THE STAR OF CHILDHOOD: a First Book of Prayers and Instruction for Children. Compiled by a Priest. With Illustrations. 16mo. 2s. 6d.

MEDITATIONS ON THE LIFE AND MYSTERIES OF OUR LORD AND SAVIOUR JESUS CHRIST. From the French. By the Compiler of 'The Treasury of Devotion.' *Crown 8vo.*

Vol. I.—THE HIDDEN LIFE OF OUR LORD. 3s. 6d.
Vol. II.—THE PUBLIC LIFE OF OUR LORD. 2 Parts. 5s. *each.*
Vol. III.—THE SUFFERING AND GLORIFIED LIFE. 3s. 6d.

SELF-RENUNCIATION. From the French. 16mo. 2s. 6d.

MAXIMS AND GLEANINGS FROM THE WRITINGS OF T. T. CARTER, M.A. Selected and arranged for Daily Use. By C. M. S. *Crown 16mo.* 1s.

NICHOLAS FERRAR : his Household and his Friends. With Portrait engraved after a Picture by CORNELIUS JANSSEN at Magdalene College, Cambridge. *Crown 8vo. 6s.*

Chandler.—THE SPIRIT OF MAN : An Essay in Christian Philosophy. By the Rev. A. CHANDLER, M.A., Rector of Poplar, E., Fellow and Late Tutor of Brasenose College, Oxford. *Crown 8vo.* 5s.

COMMON PRAYER (THE BOOK OF). Edited and arranged for the use of Children. With Texts and Proverbs. Illustrated with Photographs. 18mo. 3s. 6d.

Compton.—THE ARMOURY OF PRAYER. A Book of Devotion. Compiled by the Rev. BERDMORE COMPTON, M.A., sometime Vicar of All Saints', Margaret Street. 18mo. 3s. 6d.

Conder.—A HANDBOOK TO THE BIBLE : or, Guide to the Study of the Holy Scriptures, derived from Ancient Monuments and Modern Exploration. By F. R. CONDER, and Lieut. C. R. CONDER, R.E. *Post 8vo.* 7s. 6d.

Conybeare and Howson.—THE LIFE AND EPISTLES OF
ST. PAUL. By the Rev. W. J. CONYBEARE, M.A., and the Very
Rev. J. S. HOWSON, D.D. With numerous Maps and Illustrations.
LIBRARY EDITION. *Two Vols. 8vo. 21s.*
STUDENTS' EDITION. *One Vol. Crown 8vo. 6s.*
POPULAR EDITION. *One Vol. Crown 8vo. 3s. 6d.*

Copleston.—BUDDHISM—PRIMITIVE AND PRESENT IN
MAGADHA AND IN CEYLON. By REGINALD STEPHEN COPLE-
STON, D.D., Bishop of Colombo, President of the Ceylon Branch of
the Royal Asiatic Society, *8vo. 16s.*

Crake.—HISTORY OF THE CHURCH UNDER THE
ROMAN EMPIRE, A.D. 30-476. ,By the Rev. A. D. CRAKE, B.A.,
Author of ' Edwy the Fair,' etc. etc. *Crown 8vo. 7s. 6d.*

Creighton.—HISTORY OF THE PAPACY DURING THE
REFORMATION. By MANDELL CREIGHTON, D.D., LL.D., Bishop
of Peterborough. *8vo. Vols. I. and II., 1378-1464. 32s. Vols. III.
and IV., 1464-1518. 24s.*

Crosse.—SERMONS preached in the Church of Holy Trinity,
Hastings, and Chichester Cathedral. By THOMAS FRANCIS CROSSE,
D.C.L., late Vicar of Holy Trinity and Rural Dean of Hastings, and
Canon Residentiary and Precentor of Chichester Cathedral. *Crown
8vo. 6s.*

Devotional Series, 16mo, Red Borders. *Each 2s. 6d.*
BICKERSTETH'S YESTERDAY, TO-DAY, AND FOR EVER.
CHILCOT'S TREATISE ON EVIL THOUGHTS.
THE CHRISTIAN YEAR.
DEVOTIONAL BIRTHDAY BOOK.
HERBERT'S POEMS AND PROVERBS.
KEMPIS' (À) OF THE IMITATION OF CHRIST.
FRANCIS DE SALES' (ST.) THE DEVOUT LIFE.
WILSON'S THE LORD'S SUPPER. *Large type.*
*TAYLOR'S (JEREMY) HOLY LIVING.
*——   ——   HOLY DYING.
                    These two in one Volume. 5s.

Devotional Series, 18mo, without Red Borders. *Each 1s.*
BICKERSTETH'S YESTERDAY, TO-DAY, AND FOR EVER.
THE CHRISTIAN YEAR.
KEMPIS' (À) OF THE IMITATION OF CHRIST.
HERBERT'S POEMS AND PROVERBS.
WILSON'S THE LORD'S SUPPER. *Large type.*
FRANCIS DE SALES' (ST.) THE DEVOUT LIFE.
*TAYLOR'S (JEREMY) HOLY LIVING.
*——   ——   HOLY DYING.
                    These two in one Volume. 2s. 6d.

Dix.—THE SACRAMENTAL SYSTEM CONSIDERED AS THE EXTENSION OF THE INCARNATION : being the Bishop Paddock Lectures, delivered 1892. By MORGAN DIX, D.D., Rector of Trinity Church, New York. *Crown 8vo.* 6s.

Dutton.—THE DISCIPLINE OF LIFE. Being Last Words of Counsel, by the Rev. REGINALD G. DUTTON, M.A., sometime Curate of St. Martin's-in-the-Fields. With a Preface by the Right Rev. the BISHOP OF LICHFIELD. *Crown 8vo.* 2s. 6d.

Edersheim.—Works by ALFRED EDERSHEIM, M.A., D.D., Ph.D., sometime Grinfield Lecturer on the Septuagint in the University of Oxford.

THE LIFE AND TIMES OF JESUS THE MESSIAH. *Two Vols.* 8vo. 24s.

JESUS THE MESSIAH : being an Abridged Edition of ' The Life and Times of Jesus the Messiah.' With a Preface by the Rev. W. SANDAY, D.D., Ireland Professor of Exegesis at Oxford. *Crown 8vo.* 7s. 6d.

PROPHECY AND HISTORY IN RELATION TO THE MESSIAH : The Warburton Lectures, 1880-1884. 8vo. 12s.

A HISTORY OF THE JEWISH NATION. New Edition, Revised by H. A. WHITE, B.A., Fellow of New College, Oxford.
[In preparation.

Edwards.—WALES AND THE WELSH CHURCH. By HENRY T. EDWARDS, M.A., late Dean of Bangor. With a Biographical Sketch of the Author. With Portrait. *Crown 8vo.* 3s. 6d.

Ellicott.—Works by C. J. ELLICOTT, D.D., Bishop of Gloucester and Bristol.

A CRITICAL AND GRAMMATICAL COMMENTARY ON ST. PAUL'S EPISTLES. Greek Text, with a Critical and Grammatical Commentary, and a Revised English Translation. 8vo.

1 CORINTHIANS. 16s.	PHILIPPIANS, COLOSSIANS, AND
GALATIANS. 8s. 6d.	PHILEMON. 10s. 6d.
EPHESIANS. 8s. 6d.	THESSALONIANS. 7s. 6d.
PASTORAL EPISTLES. 10s. 6d.	

HISTORICAL LECTURES ON THE LIFE OF OUR LORD JESUS CHRIST. 8vo. 12s.

A 2

Epochs of Church History. Edited by MANDELL CREIGHTON, D.D., Bishop of Peterborough. *Small 8vo.* 2s. 6d. each.

THE ENGLISH CHURCH IN OTHER LANDS. By the Rev. H. W. TUCKER, M.A.

THE HISTORY OF THE RE-FORMATION IN ENGLAND. By the Rev. GEO. G. PERRY, M.A.

THE CHURCH OF THE EARLY FATHERS. By the Rev. ALFRED PLUMMER, D.D.

THE EVANGELICAL REVIVAL IN THE EIGHTEENTH CENTURY. By the Rev. J. H. OVERTON, M.A.

THE UNIVERSITY OF OXFORD. By the Hon. G. C. BRODRICK, D.C.L.

THE UNIVERSITY OF CAM-BRIDGE. By J. BASS MULLINGER, M.A.

THE ENGLISH CHURCH IN THE MIDDLE AGES. By the Rev. W. HUNT, M.A.

THE CHURCH AND THE EASTERN EMPIRE. By the Rev. H. F. TOZER, M.A.

THE CHURCH AND THE ROMAN EMPIRE. By the Rev. A. CARR.

THE CHURCH AND THE PURI-TANS, 1570-1660. By HENRY OFFLEY WAKEMAN, M.A.

HILDEBRAND AND HIS TIMES. By the Rev. W. R. W. STEPHENS, M.A.

THE POPES AND THE HOHEN-STAUFEN. By UGO BALZANI.

THE COUNTER-REFORMATION. By ADOLPHUS WILLIAM WARD, Litt. D.

WYCLIFFE AND MOVEMENTS FOR REFORM. By REGINALD L. POOLE, M.A.

THE ARIAN CONTROVERSY. By H. M. GWATKIN, M.A.

Ferrar.—NICHOLAS FERRAR : his Household and his Friends. With a Preface by the Rev. T. T. CARTER, M.A., Hon. Canon of Christ Church, Oxford. With Portrait engraved after a Picture by CORNELIUS JANSSEN at Magdalene College, Cambridge. *Crown 8vo.* 6s.

Ffoulkes.—A HISTORY OF THE CHURCH OF ST. MARY THE VIRGIN, Oxford, the University Church, from Domesday to the Installation of the Duke of Wellington as Chancellor. By its present Vicar, EDMUND S. FFOULKES, M.A. 10s. 6d.

'Fidelis.'—Works by 'FIDELIS.'

'QUIT YOU LIKE MEN'; for Young Men after their Confirmation. *32mo. Paper cover,* 1d. ; *limp cloth,* 3d.

HOLY COMMUNION. Invitation and simple preparation. *32mo. Paper cover,* 2d. ; *limp cloth,* 4d. *Superior Edition, cloth, gilt or red edges,* 9d.

'THINE FOR EVER'; for Girls after their Confirmation. *32mo. Paper cover,* 1d. ; *limp cloth,* 3d.

QUIET WORDS. A Volume of Addresses. *Crown 8vo. Paper cover,* 6d. ; *cloth,* 1s.

IN SICKNESS AND SUFFERING. Readings, Prayers, and Hymns. *Crown 8vo. Paper cover,* 6d. ; *cloth,* 1s.

Fosbery.—Works edited by the Rev. THOMAS VINCENT FOSBERY M.A., sometime Vicar of St. Giles's, Reading.

VOICES OF COMFORT. *Cheap Edition. Small 8vo. 3s. 6d.*
    The Larger Edition (7s. 6d.) may still be had.

HYMNS AND POEMS FOR THE SICK AND SUFFERING. In connection with the Service for the Visitation of the Sick. Selected from Various Authors. *Small 8vo. 3s. 6d.*

Gant.—THE LORD OF HUMANITY ; or, The Testimony of Human Consciousness. By FREDERICK JAMES GANT, F.R.C.S., Consulting Surgeon to the Royal Free Hospital. *Crown 8vo. 2s. 6d.*

Garland.—THE PRACTICAL TEACHING OF THE APO-CALYPSE. By the Rev. G. V. GARLAND, M.A., Rector of Binstead, Isle of Wight. *8vo. 16s.*

Gedge.—THE YOUNG CHURCHMAN'S COMPANION TO THE PRAYER-BOOK. Edited by J. W. GEDGE, M.A., Rector of St. Anthony's, Stepney. *1s. 6d.; Paper Cover, 1s.; or in Three Parts, 6d. each.*

    Part I.   Morning and Evening Prayer, and Litany.
    Part II. Baptismal and Confirmation Services.
    Part III. The Holy Communion.

Gore.—Works by the Rev. CHARLES GORE, M.A., Principal of the Pusey House, Oxford.

THE MINISTRY OF THE CHRISTIAN CHURCH. *8vo. 10s. 6d.*
ROMAN CATHOLIC CLAIMS. *Crown 8vo. 3s. 6d.*

Goulburn.—Works by EDWARD MEYRICK GOULBURN, D.D., D.C.L., sometime Dean of Norwich.

THOUGHTS ON PERSONAL RELIGION : being a treatise on the Christian Life in its Two Chief Elements, Devotion and Practice. *Small 8vo. 6s. 6d. Cheap Edition. 3s. 6d. Presentation Edition. 2 vols. small 8vo. 10s. 6d.*

THE PURSUIT OF HOLINESS : a Sequel to 'Thoughts on Personal Religion.' *Small 8vo. 5s. Cheap Edition. 3s. 6d.*

SHORT DEVOTIONAL FORMS, for Morning, Night, and Midnight, and for the Third, Sixth, Ninth Hours, and Eventide of each Day of the Week. *32mo. 1s. 6d.*

THE CHILD SAMUEL : a Practical and Devotional Commentary on the Birth and Childhood of the Prophet Samuel, as recorded in 1 Sam. i., ii. 1-27, iii. *Small 8vo. 2s. 6d.*

[continued.

Goulburn.—Works by EDWARD MEYRICK GOULBURN, D.D., D.C.L., sometime Dean of Norwich—*continued.*

THE GOSPEL OF THE CHILDHOOD : a Practical and Devotional Commentary on St. Luke ii. 41 to the end. *Crown 8vo.* 2s. 6d.

THE ACTS OF THE DEACONS: being a Commentary, Critical and Practical, upon the Notices of St. Stephen and St. Philip the Evangelist, contained in the Acts of the Apostles. *Small 8vo.* 6s.

AN INTRODUCTION TO THE DEVOTIONAL STUDY OF THE HOLY SCRIPTURES. *Small 8vo.* 6s. 6d.

THE COLLECTS OF THE DAY: an Exposition, Critical and Devotional, of the Collects appointed at the Communion. With Preliminary Essays on their Structure, Sources, and General Character. 2 vols. *Crown 8vo.* 8s. each. *Sold separately.*

THOUGHTS UPON THE LITURGICAL GOSPELS for the Sundays, one for each day in the year. 2 vols. *Crown 8vo.* 16s.

MEDITATIONS UPON THE LITURGICAL GOSPELS for the Minor Festivals of Christ, the two first Week-days of the Easter and Whitsun Festivals, and the Red-letter Saints' Days. *Crown 8vo.* 8s. 6d.

FAMILY PRAYERS, arranged on the Liturgical Principle. *Crown 8vo.* 3s. 6d. *Cheap Edition.* 16mo. 1s.

A COMMENTARY, EXPOSITORY AND DEVOTIONAL, on the Order of the Administration of the Lord's Supper, according to the Use of the Church of England ; to which is added an Appendix on Fasting Communion, etc. *Small 8vo.* 6s. *Cheap Edition,* 3s. 6d.

EVERLASTING PUNISHMENT. Lectures delivered at St. James's Church, Piccadilly. With Three Dissertations. *Crown 8vo.* 6s. 6d.

HOLY WEEK IN NORWICH CATHEDRAL : being Seven Lectures on the several Members of the Most Sacred Body of Our Lord Jesus Christ. Delivered in Norwich Cathedral. *Crown 8vo.* 5s.

THE HOLY CATHOLIC CHURCH ; its Divine Ideal, Ministry, and Institutions. With a Catechism on each Chapter. *Crown 8vo.* 6s. 6d.

A MANUAL OF CONFIRMATION. With a Pastoral Letter instructing Catechumens how to prepare themselves for their first Communion. *Small 8vo.* 1s. 6d.

Granger.—LIFE RENEWED : A Manual for Convalescence. Arranged for Daily Reading and Meditation for a Month. By M. E. GRANGER. With a Preface by the Right Rev. E. R. WILBERFORCE, D.D., Bishop of Newcastle-on-Tyne. *Small 8vo. 3s. 6d.*

Green.—THE WITNESS OF GOD AND FAITH: Two Lay Sermons. By THOMAS HILL GREEN, late Whyte's Professor of Moral Philosophy in the University of Oxford. *Fcap. 8vo. 2s.*

Gurnhill. —A COMPANION TO THE PSALTER. Consisting of Brief Introductions, Notes, and Meditations. Contributed as a Help to the Devotional Use of the Psalms in Daily Public and Private Worship. By the Rev. J. GURNHILL, B.A., Vicar of East Stockwith, and Diocesan Inspector for the Isle of Axholme. *Small 8vo. 4s.*

Harrison.—Works by the Rev. ALEXANDER J. HARRISON, B.D., Vicar of Lightcliffe, Lecturer of the Christian Evidence Society.

PROBLEMS OF CHRISTIANITY AND SCEPTICISM; Lessons from Twenty Years' Experience in the Field of Christian Evidence. *Crown 8vo. 7s. 6d.*

THE CHURCH IN RELATION TO SCEPTICS: a Conversational Guide to Evidential Work. *Crown 8vo. 7s. 6d.*

Hatch.—THE ORGANIZATION OF THE EARLY CHRISTIAN CHURCHES. Being the Bampton Lectures for 1880. By EDWIN HATCH, M.A., D.D., late Reader in Ecclesiastical History in the University of Oxford. *8vo. 5s.*

Heygate.—THE GOOD SHEPHERD ; or, Meditations for the Clergy upon the Example and Teaching of Christ. By the Rev. W. E. HEYGATE, M.A., Hon. Canon of Winchester. *Small 8vo. 3s.*

Hockin.—JOHN WESLEY AND MODERN METHODISM. By the Rev. FREDERICK HOCKIN, M.A., Rector of Phillack, Hon. Canon of Truro, and Proctor in Convocation. *Crown 8vo. 2s. 6d.*

Holland.—Works by the Rev. HENRY SCOTT HOLLAND, M.A., Canon and Precentor of St. Paul's.

PLEAS AND CLAIMS FOR CHRIST. *Crown 8vo. 7s. 6d.*

CREED AND CHARACTER : Sermons. *Crown 8vo. 3s. 6d.*

ON BEHALF OF BELIEF. Sermons preached in St. Paul's Cathedral. *Crown 8vo. 3s. 6d.*

CHRIST OR ECCLESIASTES. Sermons preached in St. Paul's Cathedral. *Crown 8vo. 3s. 6d.*

GOOD FRIDAY. Being Addresses on the Seven Last Words. Delivered at St. Paul's Cathedral on Good Friday. *Small 8vo. 2s.*

LOGIC AND LIFE, with other Sermons. *Crown 8vo. 3s. 6d.*

Hook.—A BOOK OF FAMILY PRAYER. Compiled by
WALTER FARQUHAR HOOK, D.D., F.R.S., late Dean of Chichester.
With Rubrics in Red. 18*mo.* 2*s.*

Hopkins.—CHRIST THE CONSOLER. A Book of Comfort
for the Sick. By ELLICE HOPKINS. *Small 8vo.* 2*s. 6d.*

Howard.—THE SCHISM BETWEEN THE ORIENTAL
AND WESTERN CHURCHES. With special reference to the
addition of the *Filioque* to the Creed. By the Rev. G. B. HOWARD,
B.A., sometime Scholar of St. John's College, Cambridge. *Crown 8vo.*
3*s. 6d.*

Ingram.—HAPPINESS IN THE SPIRITUAL LIFE; or, 'The
Secret of the Lord.' A Series of Practical Considerations. By W.
CLAVELL INGRAM, D.D., Dean of Peterborough. *Crown 8vo.* 7*s. 6d.*

INHERITANCE OF THE SAINTS; or, Thoughts on the
Communion of Saints and the Life of the World to come. Col-
lected chiefly from English Writers by L. P. With a Preface by the
Rev. H. S. HOLLAND, M.A., Canon and Precentor of St. Paul's. *Crown
8vo.* 7*s. 6d.*

Jacob.—Works by EDITH S. JACOB.

THE GATE OF PARADISE. A Dream of Easter Eve. 16*mo.* *Paper
cover,* 6*d.*; *cloth,* 1*s.*

THE VISION OF THE HOLY CHILD. An Allegory. *Sq.* 16*mo.* 1*s. 6d.*

James.—COMMENT UPON THE COLLECTS appointed to
be used in the Church of England on Sundays and Holy Days
throughout the Year. By JOHN JAMES, D.D., sometime Canon of
Peterborough. *Small 8vo.* 3*s. 6d.*

Jameson.—Works by Mrs. JAMESON.

SACRED AND LEGENDARY ART, containing Legends of the Angels
and Archangels, the Evangelists, the Apostles, the Doctors of the Church,
St. Mary Magdalene, the Patron Saints, the Martyrs, the Early Bishops,
the Hermits, and the Warrior-Saints of Christendom, as represented in
the Fine Arts. With 19 etchings on Copper and Steel, and 187 Woodcuts. *Two Vols. Cloth, gilt top,* 20*s. net.*

LEGENDS OF THE MONASTIC ORDERS, as represented in the
Fine Arts, comprising the Benedictines and Augustines, and Orders
derived from their Rules, the Mendicant Orders, the Jesuits, and the
Order of the Visitation of St. Mary. With 11 etchings by the Author,
and 88 Woodcuts. *One Vol. Cloth, gilt top,* 10*s. net.*

[continued.

Jameson.—Works by Mrs. JAMESON—*continued.*

LEGENDS OF THE MADONNA, OR BLESSED VIRGIN MARY.
Devotional with and without the Infant Jesus, Historical from the Annunciation to the Assumption, as represented in Sacred and Legendary Christian Art. With 27 Etchings and 165 Woodcuts. *One Vol. Cloth, gilt top,* 10s. *net.*

THE HISTORY OF OUR LORD, as exemplified in Works of Art, with that of His Types, St. John the Baptist, and other Persons of the Old and New Testament. Commenced by the late Mrs. JAMESON ; continued and completed by LADY EASTLAKE. With 31 Etchings and 281 Woodcuts. *Two Vols.* 8vo. 20s. *net.*

Jennings.—ECCLESIA ANGLICANA. A History of the Church of Christ in England from the Earliest to the Present Times. By the Rev. ARTHUR CHARLES JENNINGS, M.A., Jesus College, Cambridge. *Crown 8vo.* 7s. 6d.

Jukes.—Works by the Rev. ANDREW JUKES.

THE NEW MAN AND THE ETERNAL LIFE. Notes on the Reiterated Amens of the Son of God. *Crown 8vo.* 6s.

THE NAMES OF GOD IN HOLY SCRIPTURE : a Revelation of His Nature and Relationships. *Crown 8vo.* 4s. 6d.

THE TYPES OF GENESIS. *Crown 8vo.* 7s. 6d.

THE SECOND DEATH AND THE RESTITUTION OF ALL THINGS. *Crown 8vo.* 3s. 6d.

THE MYSTERY OF THE KINGDOM. *Crown 8vo.* 2s. 6d.

Keble.—THE CHRISTIAN YEAR. By the Rev. JOHN KEBLE, M.A.

1. Large-Type Edition. *Crown 8vo.* 3s. 6d.
2. Foolscap Edition. *With red borders. Small 8vo.* 5s.
3. Red Line Edition. *On toned Paper.* 16mo. 2s. 6d.
4. Cheap Edition. 18mo. 1s.
5. 'Aids to the Inner Life' Edition. *With red borders.* 18mo. 2s.
6. The same, *without red borders.* 32mo. 1s. ; or cloth limp, 6d.

MAXIMS AND GLEANINGS FROM THE WRITINGS OF JOHN KEBLE, M.A. Selected and Arranged for Daily Use. By C. M. S. *Crown 16mo.* 1s.

SELECTIONS FROM THE WRITINGS OF JOHN KEBLE, M.A. *Crown 8vo.* 3s. 6d.

Kempis.—OF THE IMITATION OF CHRIST. By Thomas à Kempis. A New Translation.

  1. Large Type Edition. *Crown 8vo. 3s. 6d.*
  2. Foolscap Edition. Forming a Volume of the Library of Spiritual Works for English Catholics. *Small 8vo. 5s.*
  3. 16mo Edition. Forming a Volume of the Library of Spiritual Works for English Catholics. *Cheap Edition. 2s. 6d.*
  4. Red Line Edition. *On toned Paper. 16mo. 2s. 6d.*
  5. Cheap Edition. *Without the red borders, 1s.*
  6. 'Aids to the Inner Life' Edition. Translated by the Rev. W. H. Hutchings, M.A. *32mo. 1s. ; or in cloth limp, 6d. With red borders. Royal 32mo. 2s.*

Kennaway.—CONSOLATIO ; OR, COMFORT FOR THE AFFLICTED. Edited by the late Rev. C. E. Kennaway. With a Preface by Samuel Wilberforce, D.D., late Lord Bishop of Winchester. *16mo. 2s. 6d.*

Keys to Christian Knowledge.

    Seven vols. Small 8vo. 1s. 6d. each. Sold separately.
    The 2s. 6d. Edition may still be had.

Edited by the Rev. John Henry Blunt, D.D.

A Key to the Knowledge and Use of the Holy Bible.

A Key to the Book of Common Prayer.

A Key to Church History (Ancient).

A Key to Church History (Modern).

A Key to Christian Doctrine and Practice (founded on the Church Catechism).

By John Pilkington Norris, D.D., late Archdeacon of Bristol.

A Key to the Narrative of the Four Gospels.

A Key to the Narrative of the Acts of the Apostles.

King.—DR. LIDDON'S TOUR IN EGYPT AND PALESTINE IN 1886. Being Letters descriptive of the Tour, written by his Sister, Mrs. King. *Crown 8vo. 5s.*

Knox Little.—Works by W. J. Knox Little, M.A., Canon Residentiary of Worcester, and Vicar of Hoar Cross.

SKETCHES IN SUNSHINE AND STORM: a Collection of Miscellaneous Essays and Notes of Travel. *Crown 8vo. 7s. 6d.*

THE CHRISTIAN HOME: Its Foundation and Duties. *Crown 8vo. 6s. 6d.*

THE HOPES AND DECISIONS OF THE PASSION OF OUR MOST HOLY REDEEMER. *Crown 8vo. 3s. 6d.*

[continued.

Knox Little.—Works by W. J. KNOX LITTLE, M.A., Canon Residentiary of Worcester, and Vicar of Hoar Cross—*continued.*

CHARACTERISTICS AND MOTIVES OF THE CHRISTIAN LIFE. Ten Sermons preached in Manchester Cathedral, in Lent and Advent, 1887. *Crown 8vo. 3s. 6d.*

THE LIGHT OF LIFE. Sermons preached on Various Occasions. *Crown 8vo. 3s. 6d.*

SUNLIGHT AND SHADOW IN THE CHRISTIAN LIFE. Sermons preached for the most part in America. *Crown 8vo. 3s. 6d.*

SERMONS PREACHED FOR THE MOST PART IN MANCHESTER. *Crown 8vo. 3s. 6d.*

THE MYSTERY OF THE PASSION OF OUR MOST HOLY REDEEMER. *Crown 8vo. 3s. 6d.*

THE WITNESS OF THE PASSION OF OUR MOST HOLY REDEEMER. *Crown 8vo. 3s. 6d.*

THE THREE HOURS' AGONY OF OUR BLESSED REDEEMER. Being Addresses in the form of Meditations delivered in St. Alban's Church, Manchester, on Good Friday. *Small 8vo. 2s. ; or in Paper Cover, 1s.*

Knowling.—THE WITNESS OF THE EPISTLES: a Study in Modern Criticism. By the Rev. R. J. KNOWLING, M.A., Vice-Principal of King's College, London. *8vo. 15s.*

Ladder (A) of Heaven: An Allegory in Verse. With Preface by the LORD BISHOP OF LINCOLN. *Crown 8vo. 3s. 6d.*

Lear.—Works by, and Edited by, H. L. SIDNEY LEAR.

CHRISTIAN BIOGRAPHIES. *Nine Vols. Crown 8vo. 3s. 6d. each.*

MADAME LOUISE DE FRANCE, Daughter of Louis XV., known also as the Mother Térèse de St. Augustin.

A DOMINICAN ARTIST: a Sketch of the Life of the Rev. Père Besson, of the Order of St. Dominic.

HENRI PERREYVE. By A. GRATRY. *With Portrait.*

ST. FRANCIS DE SALES, Bishop and Prince of Geneva.

A CHRISTIAN PAINTER OF THE NINETEENTH CENTURY ; being the Life of Hippolyte Flandrin.

THE REVIVAL OF PRIESTLY LIFE IN THE SEVENTEENTH CENTURY IN FRANCE.

BOSSUET AND HIS CONTEMPORARIES.

FÉNELON, ARCHBISHOP OF CAMBRAI.

HENRI DOMINIQUE LACORDAIRE.

FOR DAYS AND YEARS. A Book containing a Text, Short Reading, and Hymn for Every Day in the Church's Year. *16mo. 2s. 6d. Also a Cheap Edition, 32mo. 1s.; or cloth gilt, 1s. 6d.*

[continued.

Lear.—Works by, and Edited by, H. L. SIDNEY LEAR—*continued.*

FIVE MINUTES. Daily Readings of Poetry. 16mo. 3s. 6d. *Also a Cheap Edition.* 32mo. 1s.; *or cloth gilt,* 1s. 6d.

WEARINESS. A Book for the Languid and Lonely. *Large Type. Small 8vo.* 5s.

THE LIGHT OF THE CONSCIENCE. With an Introduction by the Rev. T. T. CARTER, M.A. 16mo. 2s. 6d. 32mo. 1s. *cloth,* 6d. *limp.*

MAIGRE COOKERY. 16mo. 2s.

DEVOTIONAL WORKS. Edited by H. L. SIDNEY LEAR. *Nine Vols.* 16mo. 2s. 6d. *each.*

SPIRITUAL LETTERS TO MEN. By Archbishop Fénelon.

SPIRITUAL LETTERS TO WOMEN. By Archbishop Fénelon.

A SELECTION FROM THE SPIRITUAL LETTERS OF ST. FRANCIS DE SALES, Bishop and Prince of Geneva. *Cheap Edition.* 32mo. 6d. *cloth limp;* 1s. *cloth boards; or* 2s. *with red-line borders.*

A SELECTION FROM PASCAL'S 'THOUGHTS.'

THE HIDDEN LIFE OF THE SOUL.

THE SPIRIT OF ST. FRANCIS DE SALES, Bishop and Prince of Geneva.

THE LIGHT OF THE CONSCIENCE. With an Introduction by the Rev. T. T. CARTER, M.A. *Cheap Edition.* 32mo. 6d. *cloth limp;* 1s. *cloth boards.*

SELF-RENUNCIATION. From the French. With an Introduction by the Rev. T. T. CARTER, M.A.

OF THE LOVE OF GOD. By St. Francis de Sales.

Library of Spiritual Works for English Catholics. *Original Edition. With Red Borders. Small 8vo.* 5s. *each. New and Cheaper Editions.* 16mo. 2s. 6d. *each.*

OF THE IMITATION OF CHRIST. *In Four Books. A New Translation.*

THE SPIRITUAL COMBAT: together with the Supplement and the Path of Paradise. By LAURENCE SCUPOLI. *A New Translation.*

OF THE LOVE OF GOD. By ST. FRANCIS DE SALES. *A New Translation.*

THE DEVOUT LIFE. By ST. FRANCIS DE SALES. Bishop and Prince of Geneva. *A New Translation.*

THE CONFESSIONS OF ST. AUGUSTINE. *In Ten Books. A New Translation.*

THE CHRISTIAN YEAR. 5s. *Edition only. (For other editions see p.* 15.)

Liddell.—THE GOLDEN CENSER : being a Selection from the Prayers of the Saints, A.D. 69-1890. With Notes and Indices by Mrs. EDWARD LIDDELL. *Crown 8vo. 3s. 6d.*

Liddon.—Works by HENRY PARRY LIDDON, D.D., D.C.L.,' LL.D.

ESSAYS AND ADDRESSES : Lectures on Buddhism—Lectures on the Life of St. Paul—Papers on Dante. *Crown 8vo. 5s.*

THE EPISTLE TO THE ROMANS. 8vo. *[In the press.*

THE DIVINITY OF OUR LORD AND SAVIOUR JESUS CHRIST. Being the Bampton Lectures for 1866. *Crown 8vo. 5s.*

ADVENT IN ST. PAUL'S. Sermons bearing chiefly on the Two Comings of our Lord. *Two Vols. Crown 8vo. 3s. 6d. each. Cheap Edition in one Volume. Crown 8vo. 5s.*

CHRISTMASTIDE IN ST. PAUL'S. Sermons bearing chiefly on the Birth of our Lord and the End of the Year. *Crown 8vo. 5s.*

PASSIONTIDE SERMONS. *Crown 8vo. 5s.*

EASTER IN ST. PAUL'S. Sermons bearing chiefly on the Resurrection of our Lord. *Two Vols. Crown 8vo. 3s. 6d. each. Cheap Edition in one Volume. Crown 8vo. 5s.*

SERMONS PREACHED BEFORE THE UNIVERSITY OF OXFORD. *Two Vols. Crown 8vo. 3s. 6d. each. Cheap Edition in one Volume. Crown 8vo. 5s.*

SERMONS ON OLD TESTAMENT SUBJECTS. *Crown 8vo. 5s.*

SERMONS ON SOME WORDS OF CHRIST. *Crown 8vo. 5s.*

THE MAGNIFICAT. Sermons in St. Paul's. *Crown 8vo. 2s. 6d.*

SOME ELEMENTS OF RELIGION. Lent Lectures. *Small 8vo. 2s. 6d. ; or in paper cover, 1s. 6d.*
The Crown 8vo Edition (5s.) may still be had.

WALTER KERR HAMILTON, BISHOP OF SALISBURY. A Sketch, with Sermon. *8vo. 2s. 6d.*

OF THE FIVE WOUNDS OF THE HOLY CHURCH. By ANTONIO ROSMINI. Edited, with an Introduction, by H. P. LIDDON. *Crown 8vo. 7s. 6d.*

SELECTIONS FROM THE WRITINGS OF H. P. LIDDON, D.D. *Crown 8vo. 3s. 6d.*

MAXIMS AND GLEANINGS FROM THE WRITINGS OF H. P. LIDDON, D.D. Selected and arranged by C. M. S. *Crown 16mo. 1s.*

DR. LIDDON'S TOUR IN EGYPT AND PALESTINE IN 1886. Being Letters descriptive of the Tour, written by his Sister, Mrs. KING. *Crown 8vo. 5s.*

LIGHT IN THE DWELLING; or, A Harmony of the Four
Gospels. With very short and simple remarks adapted to Reading at
Family Prayers, and arranged in 365 sections for every day in the year.
By the Author of 'The Peep of Day,' etc. Revised and corrected by a
Clergyman of the Church of England. *Crown 8vo. 6s.*

Littlehales.—THE PRYMER OR PRAYER-BOOK OF THE
LAY PEOPLE IN THE MIDDLE AGES. In English, dating about
1400 A.D. Edited by HENRY LITTLEHALES. Part I. Text. *Royal
8vo. 5s.* Part II. Collation of MSS. With Introduction. *Royal 8vo. 5s.*

Loraine.—THE BATTLE OF BELIEF : A Review of the
Present Aspects of the Conflict. By the Rev. NEVISON LORAINE,
Author of ' The Sceptic's Creed.' *Crown 8vo. 5s.*

LORD'S DAY (THE) AND THE HOLY EUCHARIST :
treated in a Series of Essays by various Writers. With a Preface by
ROBERT LINKLATER, D.D., Vicar of Holy Trinity, Stroud Green.
Crown 8vo. 5s.

Luckock.—Works by HERBERT MORTIMER LUCKOCK, D.D.,
Dean of Lichfield.

AFTER DEATH. An Examination of the Testimony of Primitive
Times respecting the State of the Faithful Dead, and their Relationship
to the Living. *Crown 8vo. 6s.*

THE INTERMEDIATE STATE BETWEEN DEATH AND
JUDGMENT. Being a Sequel to *After Death. Crown 8vo. 6s.*

FOOTPRINTS OF THE SON OF MAN, as traced by St. Mark. Being
Eighty Portions for Private Study, Family Reading, and Instruc-
tions in Church. *Two Vols. Crown 8vo. 12s. Cheap Edition in one
Vol. Crown 8vo. 5s.*

THE DIVINE LITURGY. Being the Order for Holy Communion,
Historically, Doctrinally, and Devotionally set forth, in Fifty Portions.
Crown 8vo. 6s.

STUDIES IN THE HISTORY OF THE BOOK OF COMMON
PRAYER. The Anglican Reform—The Puritan Innovations—The
Elizabethan Reaction—The Caroline Settlement. With Appendices.
Crown 8vo. 6s.

THE BISHOPS IN THE TOWER. A Record of Stirring Events
affecting the Church and Nonconformists from the Restoration to the
Revolution. *Crown 8vo. 6s.*

LYRA APOSTOLICA. Poems by J. W. BOWDEN, R. H.
FROUDE, J. KEBLE, J. H. NEWMAN, R. I. WILBERFORCE, and
I. WILLIAMS; and a Preface by CARDINAL NEWMAN. 16mo. *With
red borders.* 2s. 6d.

LYRA GERMANICA. Hymns translated from the German by
CATHERINE WINKWORTH. *Small 8vo.* 5s.

Lyttelton.—PRIVATE DEVOTIONS FOR SCHOOLBOYS;
with Rules of Conduct. By WILLIAM HENRY, Third Lord Lyttelton.
32mo. 6d.

MacColl—CHRISTIANITY IN RELATION TO SCIENCE
AND MORALS. By the Rev. MALCOLM MACCOLL, M.A., Canon
Residentiary of Ripon, and Rector of St. George's, City of London.
Crown 8vo. 6s.

Manuals of Religious Instruction. Edited by JOHN PILKING-
TON NORRIS, D.D., late Archdeacon of Bristol, and Canon Residentiary of Bristol Cathedral. *Three vols. Small 8vo.* 3s. 6d. *each.*
THE OLD TESTAMENT. | THE NEW TESTAMENT. | THE PRAYER BOOK.

Mason.—Works by A. J. MASON, D.D., Canon of Truro, formerly
Fellow of Trinity College, Cambridge.

THE FAITH OF THE GOSPEL. A Manual of Christian Doctrine.
Crown 8vo. 7s. 6d. *Cheap Edition. Crown 8vo.* 3s. 6d. *Also a
Large-Paper Edition for Marginal Notes.* 4to. 12s. 6d.

THE RELATION OF CONFIRMATION TO BAPTISM. As taught
in Holy Scripture and the Fathers. *Crown 8vo.* 7s. 6d.

Medd and Bright.—LIBER PRECUM PUBLICARUM EC-
CLESIÆ ANGLICANÆ. A GULIELMO BRIGHT, S.T.P., Ædis
Christi apud Oxon. Canonico, Historiæ Ecclesiasticæ, Professore
Regio, et PETRO GOLDSMITH MEDD, A.M., Eccles. Cath. S. Albani
Canonico Honorario, Collegii Universitatis apud Oxon. Socio Seniore.
Latine redditus. *Editio Quarta,* cum Appendice. *With Rubrics in
red. Small 8vo.* 7s. 6d.

Mercier.—OUR MOTHER CHURCH: Being Simple Talk
on High Topics. By Mrs. JEROME MERCIER. *Small 8vo.* 3s. 6d.

Meyrick.—THE DOCTRINE OF THE CHURCH OF ENGLAND ON THE HOLY COMMUNION RE-STATED AS A GUIDE AT THE PRESENT TIME. By the Rev. FREDERICK MEYRICK, M.A., Rector of Blickling, and Non-Residentiary Canon of Lincoln. With a Preface by the Right Rev. EDWARD HAROLD BROWNE, D.D., sometime Bishop of Winchester. *Crown 8vo.* 4s. 6d.

** Adopted as a text-book, and recommended for Candidates for Holy Orders in the Dioceses of York, Winchester, Bangor, Bath and Wells, Lichfield, Norwich, Peterborough, St. Davids, Southwell, etc.

Molesworth.—STORIES OF THE SAINTS FOR CHILDREN: The Black Letter Saints. By Mrs. MOLESWORTH, Author of 'The Palace in the Garden,' etc. etc. With Illustrations. *Royal 16mo.* 5s.

Moon.—THE SOUL'S INQUIRIES ANSWERED IN THE WORDS OF SCRIPTURE. Selected by G. WASHINGTON MOON. A Year-Book of Scripture Texts. *Royal 32mo.* 2s. 6d. *Cheaper Edition, without Diary. Royal 32mo. Limp,* 8d.; *cloth,* 1s. 6d.

Moore.—HOLY WEEK ADDRESSES. I. The Appeal and the Claim of Christ. II. The Words from the Cross. Delivered at St. Paul's Cathedral in Holy Week. By AUBREY L. MOORE, M.A., late Honorary Canon of Christ Church, Oxford. *Small 8vo.* 2s.

Mozley.—Works by J. B. MOZLEY, D.D., late Canon of Christ Church, and Regius Professor of Divinity in the University of Oxford.

A REVIEW OF THE BAPTISMAL CONTROVERSY. *Crown 8vo.* 7s. 6d.

ESSAYS, HISTORICAL AND THEOLOGICAL. *Two Vols.* 8vo. 24s.

EIGHT LECTURES ON MIRACLES. Being the Bampton Lectures for 1865. *Crown 8vo.* 7s. 6d.

LECTURES AND OTHER THEOLOGICAL PAPERS. 8vo. 10s. 6d.

RULING IDEAS IN EARLY AGES AND THEIR RELATION TO OLD TESTAMENT FAITH. Lectures delivered to Graduates of the University of Oxford. 8vo. 10s. 6d.

SERMONS PREACHED BEFORE THE UNIVERSITY OF OXFORD, and on Various Occasions. *Crown 8vo.* 7s. 6d.

SERMONS, PAROCHIAL AND OCCASIONAL. *Crown 8vo.* 7s. 6d.

LETTERS OF THE REV. J. B. MOZLEY, D.D. Edited by his Sister. 8vo. 12s.

Mozley.—Works by the Rev. T. MOZLEY, M.A., Author of 'Reminiscences of Oriel College and the Oxford Movement.'

THE WORD. *Crown 8vo. 7s. 6d.*

THE SON. *Crown 8vo. 7s. 6d.*

LETTERS FROM ROME ON THE OCCASION OF THE ŒCUMENICAL COUNCIL 1869-1870. *Two Vols. Cr. 8vo. 18s.*

Neale.—SELECTIONS FROM THE WRITINGS OF JOHN MASON NEALE, D.D. *Crown 8vo. 3s. 6d.*

Newbolt.—Works by the Rev. W. C. E. NEWBOLT, M.A., Canon and Chancellor of St. Paul's.

PENITENCE AND PEACE: being Addresses on the 51st and 23rd Psalms. *Crown 8vo. 2s. 6d.*

THE FRUIT OF THE SPIRIT. Being Ten Addresses bearing on the Spiritual Life. *Crown 8vo. 2s. 6d.*

THE MAN OF GOD. Being Six Addresses delivered during Lent 1886 at the Primary Ordination of the Right Rev. the Lord Alwyne Compton, D.D., Bishop of Ely. *Small 8vo. 1s. 6d.*

THE PRAYER BOOK: Its Voice and Teaching. Being Spiritual Addresses bearing on the Book of Common Prayer. *Crown 8vo. 2s. 6d.*

Newman.—Works by JOHN HENRY NEWMAN, B.D., sometime Vicar of St. Mary's, Oxford.

PAROCHIAL AND PLAIN SERMONS. Edited by the Rev. W. J. COPELAND, B.D., late Rector of Farnham, Essex. *Eight Vols. Cabinet Edition. Crown 8vo. 5s. each. Popular Edition. Eight Vols. Crown. 8vo. 3s. 6d. each.*

SELECTION, ADAPTED TO THE SEASONS OF THE ECCLE-SIASTICAL YEAR, from the 'Parochial and Plain Sermons.' Edited by the Rev. W. J. COPELAND, B.D., late Rector of Farnham, Essex. *Cabinet Edition. Crown 8vo. 5s. Popular Edition. Crown 8vo. 3s. 6d.*

FIFTEEN SERMONS PREACHED BEFORE THE UNIVERSITY OF OXFORD, between A.D. 1826 and 1843. *Cabinet Edition. Crown 8vo. 5s. Popular Edition. Crown 8vo. 3s. 6d.*

SERMONS BEARING UPON SUBJECTS OF THE DAY. Edited by the Rev. W. J. COPELAND, B.D., late Rector of Farnham, Essex. *Cabinet Edition. Crown 8vo. 5s. Popular Edition. Crown 8vo. 3s. 6d.*

(continued.

Newman.—Works by JOHN HENRY NEWMAN, B.D., sometime Vicar of St. Mary's Oxford.—*continued.*

LECTURES ON THE DOCTRINE OF JUSTIFICATION. *Cabinet Edition. Crown 8vo. 5s. Popular Edition. Crown 8vo. 3s. 6d.*

*** *For other Works by Cardinal Newman, see Messrs. Longmans & Co.'s Catalogue of Works in General Literature.*

Newnham.—Works by the Rev. P. H. NEWNHAM.

THE ALL-FATHER: Sermons preached in a Village Church. With Preface by EDNA LYALL. *Crown 8vo. 4s. 6d.*

THY HEART WITH MY HEART. Four Simple Letters on the Holy Communion. *18mo. sewed 3d. ; cloth limp 6d. ; cloth boards 8d.*

Newnham.—ALRESFORD ESSAYS FOR THE TIMES. By Rev. W. O. NEWNHAM, M.A., sometime Rector of Alresford. CONTENTS :—Bible Story of Creation—Bible Story of Eden—Bible Story of the Deluge—After Death—Miracles : A Conversation—Eternal Punishment—The Resurrection of the Body. *Crown 8vo. 6s.*

Noel.—THE NAME OF JESUS, and other Poems. By C. M. NOEL. With Memorial Notice. *Small 8vo. 2s. 6d.*

Norris.—Works by JOHN PILKINGTON NORRIS, D.D., late Archdeacon of Bristol, and Canon Residentiary of Bristol Cathedral.

RUDIMENTS OF THEOLOGY. A First Book for Students. *Crown 8vo. 7s. 6d.*

A CATECHIST'S MANUAL, in Seven Lessons on the Church Catechism. *Fcap. 8vo. 1s. 3d.*

EASY LESSONS ADDRESSED TO CANDIDATES FOR CONFIRMATION. *18mo. 1s. 6d.*

Osborne.—Works by EDWARD OSBORNE, Mission Priest of the Society of St. John the Evangelist, Cowley, Oxford.

THE CHILDREN'S SAVIOUR. Instructions to Children on the Life of our Lord and Saviour Jesus Christ. *Illustrated. 16mo. 2s. 6d.*

THE SAVIOUR-KING. Instructions to Children on Old Testament Types and Illustrations of the Life of Christ. *Illustrated. 16mo. 2s. 6d.*

THE CHILDREN'S FAITH. Instructions to Children on the Apostles' Creed. *Illustrated. 16mo. 2s. 6d.*

Oxenden.—Works by the Right Rev. ASHTON OXENDEN, formerly Bishop of Montreal.

PLAIN SERMONS, to which is prefixed a Memoir with Portrait. *Crown 8vo.*

THE HISTORY OF MY LIFE : An Autobiography. *Crown 8vo.* 5s.

PEACE AND ITS HINDRANCES. *Crown 8vo. Paper cover, 1s.; cloth, 2s.*

THE PATHWAY OF SAFETY ; or, Counsel to the Awakened. *Fcap. 8vo, large type. 2s. 6d. Cheap Edition. Cloth limp. 1s.*

THE EARNEST COMMUNICANT. 32mo, 1s. *Red Rubric Edition.* 32mo. 2s.

SHORT COMMENTS ON ST. MATTHEW AND ST. MARK. For Family Worship. *Crown 8vo. 3s. 6d.*

TOUCHSTONES ; or, Christian Graces and Characters Tested. *Fcap. 8vo. 2s. 6d.*

SHORT LECTURES ON THE SUNDAY GOSPELS. ADVENT TO EASTER. EASTER TO ADVENT. *Fcap. 8vo. 2s. 6d. each.*

THE PARABLES OF OUR LORD. *Fcap. 8vo, large type. 3s.*

PORTRAITS FROM THE BIBLE. *Two Vols.* OLD TESTAMENT. NEW TESTAMENT. *Fcap. 8vo. 2s. 6d. each.*

OUR CHURCH AND HER SERVICES. *Fcap. 8vo. 2s. 6d.*

THE CHRISTIAN LIFE. *Fcap. 8vo, large type. 2s. 6d. Cheap Edition. Small type, cloth limp. 1s.*

FAMILY PRAYERS FOR FOUR WEEKS. First Series. *Fcap. 8vo. 2s. 6d.* Second Series. *Fcap. 8vo. 2s. 6d.*

VERY LARGE TYPE EDITION. Two Series in one Volume. *Square crown 8vo. 6s.*

COTTAGE SERMONS; or, Plain Words to the Poor. *Fcap. 8vo. 2s. 6d.*

COTTAGE READINGS. *Fcap. 8vo, large type. 2s. 6d.*

THOUGHTS FOR LENT. In Seven Chapters. *Small 8vo. 1s. 6d.*

THOUGHTS FOR HOLY WEEK. 16mo. 1s. 6d.

THOUGHTS FOR ADVENT. In Nine Chapters. *Fcap. 8vo. 1s. 6d.*

[continued

Oxenden.—Works by the Right Rev. ASHTON OXENDEN, formerly Bishop of Montreal—*continued.*

DECISION. 18*mo.* 1*s.* 6*d.*

THE HOME BEYOND ; or, A Happy Old Age. *Fcap. 8vo, large type, cloth.* 1*s.* 6*d.*

GOD'S MESSAGE TO THE POOR. 18*mo, large type, cloth.* 1*s.* 6*d.*

THE LABOURING MAN'S BOOK. 18*mo, large type, cloth.* 1*s.* 6*d.*

CONFIRMATION. 18*mo, cloth.* 6*d.* ; *sewed,* 3*d.* ; *or* 2*s.* 6*d. per dozen.*

COUNSELS TO THOSE WHO HAVE BEEN CONFIRMED ; or, Now is the Time to serve Christ. 18*mo, cloth.* 1*s.*

BAPTISM SIMPLY EXPLAINED. 18*mo, cloth.* 1*s. Cheap Edition. Paper.* 6*d.*

THE LORD'S SUPPER SIMPLY EXPLAINED. 18*mo, cloth.* 1*s. Cheap Edition. Paper.* 6*d.*

PRAYERS FOR PRIVATE USE. 32*mo, cloth.* 1*s.*

FERVENT PRAYER. 18*mo, large type, limp cloth.* 1*s.*

WORDS OF PEACE ; or, The Blessings of Sickness. 16*mo.* 1*s.*

THE STORY OF RUTH. 18*mo, large type, limp cloth.* 1*s.*

A PLAIN HISTORY OF THE CHRISTIAN CHURCH. 18*mo, large type, limp cloth.* 1*s.*

GREAT TRUTHS IN VERY PLAIN LANGUAGE. 18*mo, large type, limp cloth.* 1*s.*

SHORT SERVICES FOR FAMILY WORSHIP, etc. 18*mo, sewed,* 3*d.* ; *limp cloth,* 4*d.*

THE BARHAM TRACTS. Nos. 1-49. 3*s. in Packet.*

THE PLUCKLEY TRACTS. Old Testament. Nos. 1-33. 2*s. in Packet.* New Testament. Nos. 34-67. 2*s. in Packet.*

OXFORD HOUSE PAPERS. Papers for Working Men. Written by Members of the University of Oxford. Two Series. *Crown 8vo.* 2*s.* 6*d. each.*

Paget.—Works by the Very Rev. FRANCIS PAGET, D.D., Dean of Christ Church, Oxford.

THE SPIRIT OF DISCIPLINE : Sermons. Together with an Introductory Essay concerning Accidie. *Crown 8vo.* 6*s.* 6*d.*

FACULTIES AND DIFFICULTIES FOR BELIEF AND DISBELIEF. *Crown 8vo.* 6*s.* 6*d.*

THE HALLOWING OF WORK. Addresses given at Eton, January 16-18, 1888. *Small 8vo.* 2*s.*

Percival—SOME HELPS FOR SCHOOL LIFE. Sermons preached at Clifton College, 1862-1879, by the Rev. J. PERCIVAL, M.A., LL.D., Head Master of Rugby School, and late Head Master of Clifton College. *Crown 8vo.* 7*s.* 6*d.*

PRACTICAL REFLECTIONS. By a CLERGYMAN. With
Prefaces by H. P. LIDDON, D.D., D.C.L., and the Bishop of Lincoln.
Crown 8vo.

| THE HOLY GOSPELS. 4s. 6d. | THE PSALMS. 5s. |
| ACTS TO REVELATION. 6s. | GENESIS. 4s. 6d. |

PRIEST TO THE ALTAR (THE) ; or, Aids to the Devout
Celebration of Holy Communion, chiefly after the Ancient English
Use of Sarum. *Royal 8vo.* 12s.

Puller.—THE PRIMITIVE SAINTS AND THE SEE OF
ROME. By F. W. PULLER, M.A., Mission Priest of the Society of
St. John Evangelist, Cowley, Oxford. *Crown 8vo.*

⁓Pusey.—Works by the Rev. E. B. PUSEY, D.D.
PRIVATE PRAYERS. With Preface by H. P. LIDDON, D.D., late
Chancellor and Canon of St. Paul's. *Royal 32mo.* 1s.
PRAYERS FOR A YOUNG SCHOOLBOY. With Preface by H.
P. LIDDON, D.D. 24m. 1s.
SELECTIONS FROM THE WRITINGS OF EDWARD BOUVERIE
PUSEY, D.D. *Crown 8vo.* 3s. 6d.
MAXIMS AND GLEANINGS FROM THE WRITINGS OF
EDWARD BOUVERIE PUSEY, D.D. Selected and Arranged for
Daily Use. By C. M. S. *Crown 16mo.* 1s.

Reynolds.—THE NATURAL HISTORY OF IMMORTALITY.
By the Rev. J. W. REYNOLDS, M.A., Prebendary of St. Paul's.
Crown 8vo. 7s. 6d.

Riddle.—Works by the Rev. J. E. RIDDLE, M.A.
MANUAL OF THE WHOLE SCRIPTURE HISTORY, and of the
History of the Jews between the Periods of the Old and New Testa-
ments ; including Biblical Antiquities, etc. *Small 8vo.* 4s.
OUTLINES OF SCRIPTURE HISTORY. Being an Abridgment of
the ' Manual of the Whole Scripture History.' *Small 8vo.* 2s. 6d.

St. Francis de Sales.—Works by ST. FRANCIS DE SALES, Bishop
and Prince of Geneva.
THE DEVOUT LIFE. 32mo. *Limp 6d., cloth* 1s. *With red borders,* 2s.
18mo. 1s. *With red borders,* 16mo. 2s. 6d. *Fcap 8vo.* 5s.
THE LOVE OF GOD. 16mo. 2s. 6d. *Fcap 8vo.* 5s.
SPIRITUAL LETTERS. 32mo. *Limp, 6d.; cloth* 1s.; *red borders,* 2s.
16mo. 2s. 6d.
THE SPIRIT OF ST FRANCIS DE SALES. 16mo. 2s. 6d.
THE LIFE OF ST. FRANCIS DE SALES. Edited by H. L. SIDNEY
LEAR. *Crown 8vo.* 3s. 6d.

Sanday.—Works by W. SANDAY M.A., D.D., LL.D., Dean Ireland's Professor of Exegesis and Fellow of Exeter College.

THE ORACLES OF GOD: Nine Lectures on the Nature and Extent of Biblical Inspiration and the Special Significance of the Old Testament Scriptures at the Present Time. *Crown 8vo.* 4*s*.

TWO PRESENT-DAY QUESTIONS. I. Biblical Criticism. II. The Social Movement. Sermons preached before the University of Cambridge on Ascension Day and the Sunday after Ascension Day, 1892. *Crown 8vo.* 2*s*. 6*d*.

Scudamore.—WORDS TO TAKE WITH US: A Manual of Daily and Occasional Prayers, for Private and Common Use. With Plain Instructions and Counsels on Prayer. By W. E. SCUDAMORE, M.A., late Rector of Ditchingham. *Small 8vo.* 2*s*. 6*d*.

Seebohm.—THE OXFORD REFORMERS—JOHN COLET, ERASMUS, AND THOMAS MORE: A History of their Fellow-Work. By FREDERIC SEEBOHM. *8vo.* 14*s*.

Simcox.—THE BEGINNINGS OF THE CHRISTIAN CHURCH. Lectures delivered in the Chapter-Room of Winchester Cathedral. By WILLIAM HENRY SIMCOX, M.A. *Crown 8vo.* 7*s*. 6*d*.

Stanton.—THE PLACE OF AUTHORITY IN MATTERS OF RELIGIOUS BELIEF. By VINCENT HENRY STANTON, D.D., Fellow of Trinity College, Ely Professor of Divinity in the University of Cambridge. *Crown 8vo.* 6*s*.

Stephen.—ESSAYS IN ECCLESIASTICAL BIOGRAPHY. By the Right Hon. Sir J. STEPHEN. *Crown 8vo.* 7*s*. 6*d*.

Stone.—THE KNIGHT OF INTERCESSION, and other Poems. By S. J. STONE, M.A., Pembroke College, Oxford, Vicar of All Hallows, City of London. *Crown 8vo.* 6*s*.

Swayne.—THE BLESSED DEAD IN PARADISE. Four All Saints' Day Sermons, preached in Salisbury Cathedral. By ROBERT G. SWAYNE, M.A., Chancellor and Canon Residentiary. *Crown 8vo.* 3*s*. 6*d*.

Swayne.—AN INQUIRY INTO THE NATURE OF OUR LORD'S KNOWLEDGE AS MAN. By W. S. SWAYNE, M.A. Oxon., Clerk in Holy Orders, Theological Lecturer and Diocesan Preacher in the Diocese of Lichfield. With a Preface by the Lord Bishop of SALISBURY. *Crown 8vo.* 2s.

Thornton.—FAMILY PRAYERS. By the late HENRY THORNTON, M.P. Revised and Corrected by Archdeacon HARRISON, and edited by HENRY SYKES THORNTON, Grandson of the Author. *Small 8vo.* 3s.

Tweddell.—THE SOUL IN CONFLICT. A Practical Examination of some Difficulties and Duties of the Spiritual Life. By MARSHALL TWEDDELL, M.A., Vicar of St. Saviour, Paddington. *Crown 8vo.* 6s.

Twells.—COLLOQUIES ON PREACHING. By HENRY TWELLS, M.A., Honorary Canon of Peterborough Cathedral, Rector of Waltham, Leicestershire, and Rural Dean. *Crown 8vo.* 2s. 6d.

Wakeman.—THE HISTORY OF RELIGION IN ENGLAND. By HENRY OFFLEY WAKEMAN, M.A., Fellow of All Souls College, Bursar and Tutor of Keble College, Oxford. *Small 8vo.* 1s. 6d.

Welldon. — THE FUTURE AND THE PAST. Sermons preached to Harrow Boys. By the Rev. J. E. C. WELLDON, M.A., Head Master of Harrow School. *Crown 8vo.* 7s. 6d.

Whately.—INTRODUCTORY LESSONS ON CHRISTIAN EVIDENCES. Compiled by RICHARD WHATELY, D.D. 18mo. 6d.

JOLY'S QUESTIONS on the above. *Small 8vo.* 2d.

AUDEN'S ANALYSIS of the above, with Examination Papers. 18mo. 6d.

Williams.—Works by the Rev. ISAAC WILLIAMS, B.D.

A DEVOTIONAL COMMENTARY ON THE GOSPEL NARRATIVE. *Eight Vols. Crown 8vo.* 5s. *each. Sold separately.*

THOUGHTS ON THE STUDY OF THE HOLY GOSPELS.

A HARMONY OF THE FOUR GOSPELS.

OUR LORD'S NATIVITY.

OUR LORD'S MINISTRY (Second Year).

OUR LORD'S MINISTRY (Third Year).

THE HOLY WEEK.

OUR LORD'S PASSION.

OUR LORD'S RESURRECTION.

[continued.

Williams.—Works by the Rev. ISAAC WILLIAMS, B.D., formerly Fellow of Trinity College, Oxford—*continued.*

FEMALE CHARACTERS OF HOLY SCRIPTURE. A Series of Sermons. *Crown 8vo.* 5*s.*

THE CHARACTERS OF THE OLD TESTAMENT. A Series of Sermons. *Crown 8vo.* 5*s.*

THE APOCALYPSE. With Notes and Reflections. *Crown 8vo.* 5*s.*

SERMONS ON THE EPISTLES AND GOSPELS FOR THE SUNDAYS AND HOLY DAYS THROUGHOUT THE YEAR. *Two Vols. Crown 8vo.* 5*s. each. Sold separately.*

PLAIN SERMONS ON THE CATECHISM. *Two Vols. Crown 8vo.* 5*s. each. Sold separately.*

SELECTIONS FROM THE WRITINGS OF ISAAC WILLIAMS, B.D. *Crown 8vo.* 3*s. 6d.*

THE AUTOBIOGRAPHY OF ISAAC WILLIAMS, B.D. Edited by his brother-in-law, the Venerable Sir GEORGE PREVOST, late Archdeacon of Gloucester, as throwing further light on the history of the Oxford Movement. *Crown 8vo.* 5*s.*

Woodford.—Works by JAMES RUSSELL WOODFORD, D.D., late Lord Bishop of Ely.

THE GREAT COMMISSION. Twelve Addresses on the Ordinal. Edited, with an Introduction on the Ordinations of his Episcopate, by HERBERT MORTIMER LUCKOCK, D.D., one of his examining Chaplains. *Crown 8vo.* 5*s.*

SERMONS ON OLD AND NEW TESTAMENT SUBJECTS. Edited by HERBERT MORTIMER LUCKOCK, D.D., one of his examining Chaplains. *Two Vols. Crown 8vo.* 5*s. each. Sold separately.*

Vol. I.—OLD TESTAMENT SUBJECTS.

Vol. II.—NEW TESTAMENT SUBJECTS.

Woodruff.—THE CHILDREN'S YEAR. Verses for the Sundays and Holy Days throughout the Year. By C. H. WOODRUFF, B.C.L. With an Introduction by the Lord Bishop of SOUTHWELL. *Small 8vo.* 3*s. 6d.*

Wordsworth.—Works by the late CHRISTOPHER WORDSWORTH, D.D., Bishop of Lincoln.

THE HOLY BIBLE (the Old Testament). With Notes, Introductions, and Index. *Six Vols. Imperial 8vo.* 120s. *Sold separately.*

In Parts.	£ s. d.	In Volumes.	£ s. d.
PART		VOL.	
I. Genesis and Exodus,	0 14 0	I. The Pentateuch, .	1 5 0
II. Leviticus, Numbers, Deuteronomy,	0 12 0	II. Joshua to Samuel,	0 15 0
III. Joshua, Judges, Ruth,	0 9 0		
IV. Books of Samuel,	0 7 0	III. Kings to Esther,	0 15 0
V. Kings, Chronicles, Ezra, Nehemiah, Esther,	0 15 0	IV. Job to Song of Solomon,	1 5 0
VI. Book of Job,	0 7 0		
VII. Psalms,	0 11 0	V. Isaiah to Ezekiel,	1 5 0
VIII. Proverbs, Ecclesiastes, Song of Solomon,	0 9 0		
IX. Isaiah,	0 10 0	VI. Daniel, Minor Prophets, and Index,	0 15 0
X. Jeremiah, Lamentations, Ezekiel,	0 16 0		
XI. Daniel,	0 5 0		
XII. Minor Prophets,	0 9 0		
Index,	0 2 0		
	£6 6 0		£6 0 0

THE NEW TESTAMENT, in the Original Greek. With Notes, Introductions, and Indices. *Two Vols. Imperial 8vo.* 60s. *Sold separately.*

In Parts.	£ s. d.	In Volumes.	£ s. d.
PART		VOL.	
I. Gospels,	0 16 0	I. Gospels and Acts of the Apostles,	1 3 0
II. Acts of the Apostles,	0 8 0		
III. St. Paul's Epistles,	1 3 0	II. Epistles, Apocalypse, and Indices,	1 17 0
IV. General Epistles, Apocalypse, and Index,	0 16 0		
	£3 3 0		£3 0 0

LECTURES ON INSPIRATION OF THE BIBLE. *Small 8vo.* 1s. 6d. *cloth.* 1s. *sewed.*

A CHURCH HISTORY TO A.D. 451. *Four Vols. Crown 8vo.*

Vol. I.—TO THE COUNCIL OF NICÆA, A.D. 325. 8s. 6d.
Vol. II.—FROM THE COUNCIL OF NICÆA TO THAT OF CONSTANTINOPLE. 6s.
Vol. III.—CONTINUATION. 6s.
Vol. IV.—CONCLUSION, TO THE COUNCIL OF CHALCEDON, A.D. 451. 6s.

[continued

Wordsworth.—Works by the late CHRISTOPHER WORDSWORTH, D.D., Bishop of Lincoln—*continued.*
THEOPHILUS ANGLICANUS. 12mo. 2s. 6d.
ELEMENTS OF INSTRUCTION ON THE CHURCH. 16mo. 1s. *cloth.* 6d. *sewed.*
ST. HIPPOLYTUS AND THE CHURCH OF ROME. *Crown 8vo.* 7s. 6d.
ON UNION WITH ROME. *Small 8vo.* 1s. 6d. *Sewed,* 1s.
THE HOLY YEAR: Original Hymns. 16mo. 2s. 6d. and 1s. *Limp,* 6d.
   ,,   ,,   With Music. Edited by W. H. MONK. *Square 8vo.* 4s. 6d.
GUIDES AND GOADS. (An English Edition of ' Ethica et Spiritualia.') 32mo. 1s. 6d.
MISCELLANIES, Literary and Religious. *Three Vols.* 8vo. 36s.
ON THE INTERMEDIATE STATE OF THE SOUL AFTER DEATH. 32mo. 1s.

THE LIFE OF CHRISTOPHER WORDSWORTH, D.D., Bishop of Lincoln. By JOHN HENRY OVERTON, M.A., Canon of Lincoln, and Rector of Epworth, and ELIZABETH WORDSWORTH, Principal of Lady Margaret Hall, Oxford. *With Portraits. Crown 8vo.* 7s. 6d.

Wordsworth.—Works by CHARLES WORDSWORTH, D.D., D.C.L., Bishop of St. Andrews.
ANNALS OF MY EARLY LIFE, 1806-1846. 8vo. 15s.
PRIMARY WITNESS TO THE TRUTH OF THE GOSPEL: a Series of Discourses. Also a Charge on Modern Teaching on the Canon of the Old Testament. *Crown 8vo.* 7s. 6d.

Wordsworth.—Works by ELIZABETH WORDSWORTH, Principal of Lady Margaret Hall, Oxford.
ILLUSTRATIONS OF THE CREED. *Crown 8vo.* 5s.
THE DECALOGUE. *Crown 8vo.* 4s. 6d.
ST. CHRISTOPHER AND OTHER POEMS. *Crown 8vo.* 6s.

Younghusband.—Works by FRANCES YOUNGHUSBAND.
THE STORY OF OUR LORD, told in Simple Language for Children. With 25 Illustrations on Wood from Pictures by the Old Masters, and numerous Ornamental Borders, Initial Letters, etc., from Longmans' New Testament. *Crown 8vo.* 2s. 6d.
THE STORY OF GENESIS, told in Simple Language for Children. *Crown 8vo.* 2s. 6d.
THE STORY OF THE EXODUS, told in Simple Language for Children. With Map and 29 Illustrations. *Crown 8vo.* 2s. 6d.

Printed by T. and A. CONSTABLE, Printers to Her Majesty, at the Edinburgh University Press.
10,000/2/93.

www.ingramcontent.com/pod-product-compliance
Lightning Source LLC
Chambersburg PA
CBHW020543270326
41927CB00006B/705